EDUCATION FOR DIVERSITY

Education for Diversity
Making Differences

ANDREW STABLES
University of Bath, UK

ASHGATE

Published by
Ashgate Publishing Limited
Gower House
Croft Road
Aldershot
Hampshire GU11 3HR
England

Ashgate Publishing Company
Suite 420
101 Cherry Street
Burlington, VT 05401-4405
USA

Ashgate website: http://www.ashgate.com

British Library Cataloguing in Publication Data
Stables, Andrew
  Education for diversity : making differences. - (Monitoring
  change in education)
  1. Education - Philosophy
  I. Title
  370.1

Library of Congress Cataloging-in-Publication Data
Stables, Andrew, 1956-
  Education for diversity : making differences / Andrew Stables.
      p. cm. -- (Monitoring change in education)
  Includes bibliographical references and index.
  ISBN 0-7546-3378-0
    1. Education--Philosophy. 2. Educational sociology. I. Title. II. Series.

  LB14.7 .S72 2002
  370.11'5--dc21

2002028105

ISBN 0 7546 3378 0

Printed and bound in Great Britain by
Antony Rowe Ltd., Chippenham, Wiltshire

Contents

Preface

The closing years of the twentieth century brought increasing political and media attention to the effectiveness of education, yet increasingly little, it sometimes seemed, to fundamental issues concerning it. There were exceptions, of course. For example, Nigel Blake, Paul Smeyers, Richard Smith and Paul Standish's *Thinking Again: education after postmodernism* (1998) sought both to explain the prevailing emphasis on 'performativity', and to reassure us that prevailing cultural conditions can act as a stimulus to new thinking as well as a graveyard for the old (a point made by the postmodern philosopher, Jean-Francois Lyotard, on whose work the authors drew).

In the same spirit, this book encourages a reappraisal. It has little directly to say about the effectiveness of existing procedures or policies, or how to improve them. Indeed, it is little concerned with the kind of evidence that is generally expected to inform policy and practice. Rather, it invites a reconsideration of some of the assumptions that have underpinned recent thinking about education in recent times: assumptions about children, about cultural values, and about what teaching can, and cannot, feasibly achieve. On such assumptions depend the interpretation of all evidence.

The following work is intended as a contribution to educational theory and the philosophy of education, although it does not subscribe to the sometimes fashionable view of educational theory as the province of self-reflecting practitioners, and it runs the danger of sacrificing some analytical rigour in favour of speculation over some (relatively) 'big ideas'. The approach is thus very 'broad brush', and this brings both rewards and challenges. Unlike many books about education, the sociocultural context is here seen as all important. Educational institutions are not seen as drivers of social change so much as in a dialogical relationship with the rest of society (however defined) and, as part of that dialogue, educators should be engaged in spirited debate and not merely in implementation. While practices of schooling, for example, clearly impact on the emerging social and personal identities of young people, as well as affecting their chances of gaining potentially important qualifications, schools remain conservative rather than radical forces, with social change largely driven from elsewhere. Schools did not drive the development of the information society of the late 1990s; nor did higher education, though research played its part. However, to forego discussion of such issues for easy closure, and to see educators as mere implementers of change, is to remove such influence as education can have, while to study education without attention to prevailing social and cultural conditions is to retreat into a kind of solipsism.

On the other hand, this attempt at reconsidering educational assumptions runs many risks. Many literatures are touched on in the following chapters, yet a criticism might be that few are explored in any depth, and a little learning can, indeed, be a dangerous thing. In attempting to draw together work from philosophy, sociology and elsewhere into something approaching coherence, a number of compromises have been made. Critics may sometimes be frustrated that conclusions are drawn lightly or even, on occasion, glossed over, and that questions are begged that are scarcely answered. For example, the book commends interpretation, and is much influenced by Wittgenstein's *Philosophical Investigations*, yet Wittgenstein insists that often learning does not involve interpretation. Elsewhere, Vygotsky is aligned with Piaget as a sort of stage theorist, yet this is not the common view of Vygotsky. In each case, a brief explanation of the potentially questionable position taken is given in footnotes. It would be more satisfying for all parties if such issues could all be explored in greater depth, but it would detract from the overall purpose of the work, which is not so much to prove as to provoke. The test of time may decide whether this is explanation or excuse. Either way, this is an argument that must needs indulge in some generalization.

One such generalization, underpinning the argument that is to follow, is that the past fifty years has brought significant social and cultural change. While it is a temptation of all generations to feel they are at the forefront of something new, when in fact they are merely heirs to long and slowly evolving traditions, the commentators whose ideas set the scene for the debates to follow (Beck, Giddens, Castells and others) enjoy considerable respect and influence. Their ideas deserve, if nothing else, to be considered, and this book is offered as little more than an invitation to consider them with respect to education. While the history of humankind can be read as one of slow globalization, driven by trade and the development of language and symbolic systems, the coming generation is heir to a world shaped in part by technological changes that resulted in increased travel, increased consumer choice, increased contact with other cultures and (though not in all cases) increased wealth with which to take up these new opportunities. That which can be taken for granted changes over time. In this sense, there is a danger that those who provide education will always be a step behind those who are supposed to benefit from it, particularly if educational debate pays scant attention to the big questions of its age.

Chapter 1

Education and the Triple Challenge to Modernity: the case for diversity

From a period of standardization, we should now look forward to a period of diversity. In educational terms, this means an emphasis on learning as interpretation, and on an acceptance that certain tensions, such as that between cooperation and competition, can never be fully resolved. The first chapter provides an introduction to the book as a whole by defining trends in late, or post, modernity that serve to challenge key assumptions about educational policy and practice.

Education is interpretive activity, for all participants and at all levels, and interpretation brings freedom and challenge and demands choice. However, educational policy makers have consistently failed to recognize the central role of interpretation in education, preferring totalizing solutions that can stifle the kinds of questioning and creative activity that can make educational experience meaningful, interesting, exciting and valuable. Such incomplete formulations include both the belief that education exists to 'pass down' cultural heritage, and the opposite conviction that education exists to 'promote creativity', where the creative self is seen to exist as free from historical, cultural and social context. By contrast, interpretation depends on interested engagement with histories, traditions and practices, and is always unpredictable in its outcomes. From a policy perspective, the belief that there can be a 'best practice' model for all educational institutions in all contexts is equally flawed, whether this belief is driven by ideology or by empirical evidence. Hans-Georg Gadamer has written of 'historically effected consciousness';[1] Gadamerian hermeneutics provides one of the bases on which the argument for education as diversity will be developed.

Interpretation results in diversity. Indeed, the faster contexts change, the more interpretations will differ. In recent years, there has been an increasing recognition that the world needs both biodiversity and cultural diversity, and

---

[1] Gadamer, H-G. (1999 – first published 1975) *Truth and Method*, London: Continuum. Broadly, Gadamer deals with understanding as interpretation and with history as the history of understanding, and thus itself interpretive.

that the two are interrelated.[2] For example, different cultures' ways of understanding flora lead to different uses for plants, and to the possibility of new medicines and new understandings of human physical and psychological health. However, all too often, where this has been recognized in the educational debate, it has resulted in either a glib futurism ('We must educate for the future, not the past'[3]), or, less often, an extreme conservatism ('We must return to the ways of ancient cultures'[4]), ignoring the simple fact that every move into the future is the result of elements drawn from every aspect of the past. Paradoxically, education must look backwards to go forwards: it is the spirit in which this is done that matters. The past is all we have, while the future is to be made. There is thus also an element of conservative thinking in the generally pragmatic argument that follows for education as diversity: new practices must grow organically from the conditions which preceded them and not be too strongly engineered, for the future is never quite predictable, as Richard Lewontin and others have shown in

---

[2]   The 'what is true of language and culture is true of the natural world' line of thought has been increasingly promoted in recent years, and is implicit in much of the sustainable development literature. For a fuller discussion of the justification for such thinking, see Chapter 8 of the present volume. Recent publications of some interest here include Erich Kasten (1998) *Bicultural Education in the North: ways of preserving and enhancing indigenous people's languages and traditional knowledge*, New York: Waxmann; David Harman (2002) *In Light of Our Differences: how diversity in nature and culture makes us human*, Washington, DC: Smithsonian Institute Press.

[3]   The debate surrounding the school improvement and school effectiveness movements illustrates the tension here. Contrast, for example, the extremely positive, forward looking tone of Louise Stoll and Dean Fink's (1996) *Changing our Schools: linking school effectiveness and school improvement*, Buckingham: Open University Press, with the criticality of Slee, R, Weiner, G and Tomlinson, S (eds) (1998) *School Effectiveness for Whom? Challenges to the School Effectiveness and School Improvement Movements*, London: Flamer, in which the school improvement/effectiveness movement is accused of downplaying the intractability of structural and contextual constraints on the changing of institutional cultures.

[4]   See, for example, the work of C.A. Bowers, including 'Toward an Ecological Perspective', in W. Kohli (ed.) *Critical Conversations in Philosophy of Education* (New York: Routledge), critiqued in Stables, A and Scott, W (2001) 'Post-Humanist Liberal Pragmatism? Environmental Education Out of Modernity', *Journal of Philosophy of Education* 35/2, 269–279 and, more recently, *Education for Eco-Justice and Community*, Athens: University of Georgia Press. Bowers strongly associates environmental sustainability with the cultural and community practices of pre-modern societies, and urges that these be restored as far as is possible. Stables and Scott point to the difficulty of reinstating cultural practices out of their original contexts.

their work on genetics.[5] The danger of too much emphasis on educating *for* something, whether sustainable development or social justice, is that interpretation can only be stifled by too much dedication to prescribed ends. As we seem compelled to give ourselves educational aims, let us make those aims as broad and unprescriptive as possible, by educating for diversity.

Overall, this book, therefore, should be seen as part of a move from an age of standardization, in which a narrow instrumental rationality prescribes the 'best' way forward and stifles the alternatives, to an age of diversity, in which different ways of thinking, knowing and acting are encouraged, and that acknowledges paradox.

The case for educational diversity is based on an understanding of the conditions of late (or post) modernity, as identified by a range of theorists. While commentators disagree on whether what we are now experiencing is the flowering of modernity (Giddens' 'high modernity'[6]), a change of emphasis (Beck's 'risk society'[7]) or a rejection (Lyotard's 'postmodern condition'[8]), there are several common elements in these apparently disparate analyses. These can be grouped under three broad headings:

(i)   the *individualization* of reflexivity and risk (the decline of traditional social class allegiances; the increased pressure to do your own life-planning form an early age, aided and abetted by the mass media; the invitations to deconstruct and to assert cultural differences);

(ii) the *globalization* of abstract systems (the global economy, but also the global interactivity of the Internet and other communications systems; the problematizing of traditional notions of time and place; the increasing exploitation of the mass media for political ends); and

(iii) the *ecological challenge*, with its ambivalent relationship to the modernist project, given that while the ecological crisis poses a challenge to modernity, sustainability is itself one of the grand narratives so mistrusted by postmodernists.[9] Each of these calls for the

---

5   Lewontin, R. (2000) *The Triple Helix: gene, organism and environment*, Cambridge: MA: Harvard University Press.

6   Giddens, A. (1991) *Modernity and Self-Identity: self and society in the late modern age*, Cambridge: Polity.

7   Beck, U (1992) *Risk Society: towards a new modernity*, London: Sage.

8   Lyotard, J-F (1984) *The Postmodern Condition: a report on knowledge*, Manchester: Manchester University Press.

9   According to Lyotard (above), the postmodern condition is one of 'incredulity towards metanarratives' (p. xxiv), i.e. a scepticism concerning, or rejection of the ideals of modernity, such as reason, science and progress. Lyotard is particularly critical of the claims to legitimation of science.

revitalization of a non-prescriptive, exploratory commitment to learning that can simultaneously respect traditions and challenge paradigms.

Individualization

The phrase 'individualization of risk' is, perhaps, most commonly associated with Ulrich Beck's *Risk Society* (1992), though it is an idea strongly embraced by many, though not all, recent social commentators.

At the heart of the individualization thesis is the idea that, as geographically centred, relatively immobile and largely unchanging social structures have been replaced by technologically advanced, often international 'networks', the place of the individual in society has become less taken-for-granted and secure. Thus, continuing a trend that has characterized modernity (i.e. the post-medieval period) as a whole, people have become less and less the unquestioning recipients of a role allotted to them by society, and more and more the conscious agents of their own career and lifestyle choices.

Anthony Giddens has written of the manifestations of this as a move towards a 'life politics', under which the individual feels compelled, from childhood to make active choices in areas as diverse as fashion, leisure interests, careers and political and religious beliefs.[10] By contrast, in the earlier part of the twentieth century, political and religious belief, alongside dress and career, were more widely accepted as aspects of family tradition. The concomitant expectation that voters could no longer be expected to vote along traditional social class lines was one impetus in the reform of social-democratic politics in Britain and elsewhere that Giddens and others have referred to as the Third Way.[11]

Individualization poses significant challenges to some assumptions that have underlain much educational policy and practice. Even less than in Dickens' *Hard Times*[12] are we in the position of being able to regard our students as 'empty vessels' to be stuffed full of unquestioned facts and narrowly enculturated. We cannot even rely on our old Romantic assumptions about the innocence of childhood; children can be seen increasingly as consumers of educational services. In a sense, the individualization thesis offers us the challenge of formulating an 'education after childhood'.

---

[10] Giddens, 1991, p. 9 ff. Much of *Modernity and Self-Identity* is an exploration of this theme.

[11] Giddens, A. (1999) *The Third Way: the renewal of social democracy*, Cambridge: Polity.

[12] Charles Dickens' *Hard Times* ed. Kaplan, F. and Monod, S. (2001) New York: W.W. Norton.

Globalization

In *The Third Way* (1999), Giddens acknowledges globalization, alongside individualization, as a key agent of social change. While it could be argued that *homo sapiens* is a globalizing species, given that inter-group communication and trade seem always to have been characteristic of human life, modernity has been distinctive in the increasing globalization of (what Giddens refers to as) 'abstract systems'[13]. First, there was time. The increasing ubiquity of the mechanical clock, in conjunction with the increasing standardization of what it measured, meant that time was no longer measured in terms of light and dark, and the passing of the seasons, but as a commonly shared abstraction. In a similar way, information has become increasingly abstract and globalized, so that high status knowledge is no longer that which relates to, say, local conditions for planting, but is rather that which has become globally accessible and avowedly equally applicable to all contexts. The World Wide Web is, perhaps, the most powerful manifestation of this.

Most recently, there has been a much stronger globalization of monetary systems, enhanced through the interests of huge multinational corporations, and enabled by the revolution in mass communications. It has been widely recognized that this has already had huge effects on employment patterns and may impact strongly on all forms of personal and social organization.

The consequences of globalization for educational thinking have also been undertheorized. Educational policy and planning are generally undertaken in the national context in an increasingly international world, and many of our educational assumptions – about social justice, equality of opportunity, cultural heritage – are rooted in increasingly outmoded nationalist, or statist, assumptions. While commentators disagree on the extent to which the nation state is weakened by globalization, there is no doubt that its role must be redefined. In many respects, therefore, the globalization thesis presents us with the challenge of 'education after the nation'.

The Ecological Challenge

Giddens is again among those who note that ecological, or environmental, concerns pose significant challenges to the modernist 'cast of thought', with its almost unquestioned post-Enlightenment belief in social progress through science applied as technology. That very technology is now often seen as causing problems seemingly as great as those it has been able to solve: people, for example, may live in warmer houses but breathe dirtier

---

[13] *Modernity and Self-Identity*: again, a recurrent theme.

air. The modernist project, among other assumptions, took the continued availability of natural resource for granted, whereas nowadays we feel forced to consider this an important aim.[14]

Ecological thinking has also served to make us question many of our assumptions. For example, Bill McKibben has proclaimed the complete death of wild Nature, on the grounds that no spot upon Earth has now been untouched, directly or indirectly, by human hand.[15] Coupled with this, we are, as some commentators have pointed out, caught in a 'double bind' over the ecological crisis, insofar as the means we have inherited to solve the problems – science, technology, rationality, capitalism – are its immediate causes.[16] For education, then, the ecological challenge raises fundamental questions of curriculum as well as of policy. So much for the 'natural sciences'. There are important senses in which we must now be seeking an 'education after nature'.

Each of these 'challenges to modernity' has, therefore, potentially profound implications for education which have, as yet, been underexplored. In the rest of this book, it will be argued that our response to the new uncertainties regarding nature, the nation and childhood call not for tighter stipulation and greater intra-national standardization, but rather for a cultural diversity as vibrant and full of surprises as the biodiversity argued for by the ecologists. Inspired by both John Dewey's anti-Cartesian and pragmatic concept of the unity of body and mind[17] and by Samuel Taylor Coleridge's conviction that words are 'living powers',[18] I shall argue that our being-in-the-world is most richly promoted through diverse educational practices in a climate that is tolerant, even welcoming, of paradox, practices that embrace variations arising from our differences in being in the world and in the language games we play.

The succeeding chapters focus, in various ways, on the issues detailed above. Chapters 2 and 3 consider the individualization of educational opportunity and risk, with the implications for educational markets, and for

---

[14] 'Although it might be argued that environmental protection or sustainability is a *prerequisite* for any capitalist or socialist society, given the need for both material resources and physical health, the cultural practices we have inherited are not well placed to turn this prerequisite into an aim.' Quoted from p.147 of Stables, A. and Scott, W. (1999) Environmental Education and the Discourses of Humanist Modernity: redefining critical environmental literacy, *Educational Philosophy and Theory* 31/2, 145–155.

[15] McKibben, B. (1990) *The End of Nature*, New York: Anchor.

[16] Stables and Scott, *Journal of Philosophy of Education*, 2001 (Note 4, above).

[17] John Dewey (1966) *Democracy and Education*, New York: Free Press.

[18] 'For if words are not things, they are living powers...', Samuel Taylor Coleridge, quoted on the front cover of the journal, *The Use of English*.

the positioning within them of parents, pupils and other agents, as producers, consumers and products. There is discussion of the implications for education of the 'death of childhood' implied by the superseding of the educational stage theories of Piaget (and, even, in the broadest sense, Vygotsky),[19] and of the challenges to the development of self-identity arising from the increasing intrusion of the mass media into the private sphere, and from the increasing pressure towards individualized life-planning at an early age. Chapters 4, 5 and 6 focus on policy and curriculum issues with respect to nation, culture and language. There is discussion of whether there can be any basis for educational policy if the 'grand narratives' of progress and social justice that tend to underpin it as regulative ideals are deconstructed. Issues relating to the power and technologization of discourses are considered,[20] and to the ethical and moral foundations of education in a world of instant mass communication and access to information. In Chapter 6 it is argued that cultural uncertainties lead towards a pragmatic view of educational planning based on the development of 'conditional literacies'. The two succeeding chapters (7 and 8) develop this idea with reference to education and the environment, looking critically at the possibility of an education for sustainability, given the double-bind of modernity and the ecological crisis and the discreteness and anthropocentrism of existing subject discourses. Chapter 9 focuses on the individual student, asking how teaching practices can impact on positive identity development in an increasingly uncertain world by ensuring that lessons contain 'significant events' for students. The final chapter offers an overview, arguing that whatever responses are possible to all these

---

[19] Some may object to this description of Vygotsky. It is clear that Vygotsky was not a rigid stage theorist in the sense of Piaget. He did not believe that phases of development preceded phases of instruction and learning. However, his thinking in relation to the zone of proximal development can be taken to imply a linear and hierarchical view of learning. See (1978) *Mind in Society: the development of higher psychological processes*, Cambridge, Mass.: Harvard University Press, and James Wertsch's standard study of Vygotsky: (1985) *Vygotsky and the Social Formation of Mind*, Cambridge, Mass.: Harvard University Press. According to Wertsch, Vygotsky believed in 'periods of sensitivity' yet, in his psychological studies, managed to outline only a fairly narrow view of 'learning in instruction' (pp.72–73). Rupert Wegerif has, more recently, allied Piaget and Vygotsky in terms of their monological, as opposed to dialogical, conceptions of reason. See Wegerif, R. (1998) 'Two Images of Reason in Educational Theory', *School Field* 9, 77–105.

[20] 'Technologization of discourse' is a term used by Norman Fairclough to refer to the increasing sophistication in the manipulation of language for political ends via the mass media: (1995) *Critical Discourse Analysis*, London: Longman, e.g. pp. 91–92.

challenges, they cannot be fully consensual, though they can be pluralistic, pragmatic and, in some senses, both democratic and liberal.

As has already been noted, the liberal-pragmatic educational philosophy the book as a whole attempts to help develop has a number of identifiable influences, often seen as disparate, including critical theory, political liberalism and conservatism, hermeneutics and pragmatism. As such it stands in opposition to approaches that are strongly ideological (as the term is usually understood), dogmatic and centralizing.

Although there are liberal, even conservative, elements in the argument that follows, there is also one important respect in which socially critical theory derived from Marxism is acknowledged. This concerns the power of language and other forms of cultural practice in personal and social formation. In other words, the case for diversity in education does not presuppose the complete autonomy of the human agent. The argument that follows is deeply influenced by social constructivism.

At the same time, the liberal strand in the argument comes from a conviction that, while all human practice can be seen as socially constructed, individuals remain the perceiving, if not the wholly rational agents envisaged by the eighteenth century creators of modern liberalism. Even if individuality is a fiction, it is an important one therefore. Whether we like it or not, and whether or not it is rational, we are at the centres of our own worlds, though it is fervently to be hoped that we acknowledge the subjectivity of others, thus ensuring that we proceed intersubjectively rather than solipsistically. Education should therefore seek to develop individual responsibility, for the good of society and environment, on the grounds that our choices really are made by, though not necessarily for, ourselves.

The conservative strand comes partly from this acceptance of how human beings actually make decisions and see the world, but also from the acknowledgment that change, while inevitable, is also inevitably slow. Political events of the late twentieth century show this clearly. The bringing-down of the Berlin Wall, for example, seemed to mark a moment of revolutionary change, yet the changes in quality of life for those in the former Eastern Bloc have been much slower and less sharply defined. Along with this comes the acceptance that certain tensions or paradoxes are endemic to the human condition and can never be fully resolved: for example, the tension between individual freedom and social justice.

A hermeneutic approach sees education as a process of constant interpretation and reinterpretation; pragmatism views truth as what is seen to work, and rejects the idea that abstract regulative ideals (such as truth, justice, beauty, even education) can be analyzed objectively, free from contextual considerations.

Despite this multiplicity of influences, at the heart of this pragmatic-liberal approach lie two assumptions: that knowledge is humanly constructed so is never absolute (thus the need for liberalism) and that differential valorization is both an individual and a social necessity (hence the need for pragmatism). Simply, one can see all human categorization as existing on a horizontal and a vertical plane: on the horizontal plane are differences of fact; on the vertical plane are differences of worth. Human beings inevitably make both sorts of categorization, and do so always in relation to a given, perceived context. While the postmodern writings of Lyotard and others are convincing in terms of undermining our beliefs in modernity's 'grand narratives', total relativism is an impossibility. We can only be relatively relativistic! There are always scales of individual and social value; there are always differentials of power. Applications of these assumptions in educational policy and practice are likely to have certain characteristics: on the one hand, a belief in the individual and social contruction of knowledge and understanding (i.e. broadly constructivist learning theory), and, on the other, an acceptance of both the existence and the fundamental uncertainty of power differentials in all walks of life (for example, the supposed superiority of some language forms over others). It is in the mixture of these two positions that pragmatic liberalism differs from other dominant educational philosophies.

This approach to education owes a large debt, of course, to Richard Rorty's liberal pragmatism.[21] The position taken in this book differs somewhat from that hitherto adopted by Rorty because of two essential differences in emphasis. These concern the central position of 'language games', and the questioning of humanism in Chapter 9, where pragmatic liberalism is applied to the debate about education for environmental sustainability. Rorty has not concerned himself overtly with environmental issues, and several commentators have thus seen his philosophy as inapplicable to them. It is an important element of the present argument that human responsibility must extend beyond the narrowly humanistic concerns that have the political and educational philosophies that have dominated modernity.[22]

Note: Difference and Diversity

Readers versed in postmodern philosophy will have noted that I am using 'diversity' as an aim, despite the attention to 'difference' in the work of Jacques Deleuze and others.[23] In this, I have followed the practice in

---

[21] See, for example (1980) *Philosophy and the Mirror of Nature*, Princeton, N.J.: Princeton University Press; (1982) *Consequences of Pragmatism*, Brighton: Harvester; (1998) *Truth and Progress*, Cambridge: Cambridge University Press.

[22] See Stables and Scott, *Educational Philosophy and Theory*, 1999 (Note 14).

[23] Deleuze, J. (1994) *Difference and Repetition*, London: Athlone.

environmental thought and policy discourse of seeing diversity as something generally desirable, while difference is more often value neutral. I have, however, attempted to show an awareness of the possibilities for differences in interpretation (or diverse interpretations) of this through the balancing of the book's title and subtitle. Education for diversity should make a difference!

Chapter 2

Individualizing Educational Opportunity: the learner as producer, consumer and product

In recent years, the market metaphor has dominated much thinking about education. Working with this trend, Chapter 2 positions the student as consumer, and examines some of the implications of such a position.

According to many social theorists, the latter years of the second Millennium saw changes which have resulted in a tendency towards more individualized risk-taking. Labour markets have changed rapidly, making the 'job for life' a thing of the past; global communications have problematized pre-existing notions of time, place and community; goods and services have become increasingly commodified, and consumption has increasingly replaced production as the prime concern. Taken all in all, increasingly abstract and globalized systems and institutions have left individuals isolated from traditionally relatively fixed local communities and structures, and have imposed upon them increasing demands to make continual lifestyle choices.

There are two dominant readings of the consequences of this. According to one (broadly the postmodern; certainly the poststructuralist), subjectivities have been fractured, inhibiting the development of coherent self-identities;[1] according to the other (as argued by Castells, Giddens and others), traditional communities have been replaced by a proliferation of intersubjective networks, in which individuals build their own communities with little reference to geography, kinship or even social class or occupation.[2] According to this reading, what we are experiencing is not postmodernity, but a 'new' or 'high' late modernity: what Beck refers to as a 'risk society'.[3] However, while Giddens sees this as largely a positive

---

[1] See, for example, the work of Jean Baudrillard: e.g. (1988) *Jean Baudrillard: selected writings*, Poster, M. (ed.), Cambridge: Polity.
[2] Castells, M. (1996) *The Rise of the Network Society*; (1997) *The Power of Identity*, and (1998) *End of Millennium*, all Oxford: Blackwell.
[3] Beck, U. (1992) *Risk Society: towards a new modernity*, London: Sage.

process, Castells draws a sharp distinction between the empowered and the disempowered within the network society (i.e. those for whom the network society offers endless opportunity, and those whom it entraps, and effectively excludes),[4] and Beck writes of the 'individualization of social inequality' (i.e. the disadvantage experienced by those of limited economic, social and cultural capital who are no longer able to benefit from traditional working class culture).[5] Thus, in a sense, both modernist and postmodernist perspectives on these changes pose challenges for the sustenance and development of real self- and collective identities.

Whether 'post' or 'high' modernity is what is being experienced here, the eroding of traditional loyalties, including social class allegiances, is leading to a global society in which lifestyle choices both proliferate and are increasingly not to be made by reference to the cultural norms of one's family, social class group, gender or profession. 'People like us...' becomes less and less a justification for action. This tends towards further cultural pluralism. At the same time, it can be argued (as Giddens does) that institutional globalization may have a globally cohesive social and cultural effect: Giddens effectively argues that the world is becoming one in which all are 'us' and none are 'them'. Such an optimistic view can be countered, not only by reference to the workings of language, which always defines an 'us' in terms of a 'them', but in a more extreme form, by reference to bleaker postmodernist analyses such as Baudrillard's, in which self-identity is effectively drowned in a sea of 'simulcra': recycled images standing ultimately for nothing but themselves, the tendency of which is alienating.[6]

Whichever scenario is preferred, the child of the early Third Millennium is growing up in a world shaped, to some degree, by the social and cultural changes summarized above. This is a world, in part at least, in which decision-making will be highly individualized compared to a century earlier. Young people will be expected to make lifestyle choices, some of them involving significant skills of life-planning, at an early age, among options that simply did not present themselves to young people fifty years ago. At the same time, the securities of traditional allegiances of social class and gender, perhaps of the nuclear family, will not be present. Out of the traditions of class-based politics is emerging a politics of lifestyle, in which increasingly the individual becomes her own representative.

What does this mean for the school or college student? It means above all a culture of enforced and increasing choice as well as inevitable

---

[4] *The Rise of the Network Society* (Note 2).
[5] Beck, 1992, p. 92.
[6] (Note 1).

interpretation and, along with that, the existential problems of all those who, in Sartre's terms, are 'doomed to be free'.[7]

Educational Choice and Educational Markets

Debates about educational choice since the 1980s have been couched in the language of the market, despite enduring arguments concerning the degree to which education (and particularly schooling) should be emphasized as private service or as public good.[8] The market metaphor now seems firmly established in education, regardless of positions on this apparently fundamental issue.

Objections to educational markets have essentially been of three sorts: the first, touched on above, that education has a broad community function that market mechanisms are inadequate to satisfy; the second that the market in schools (where attendance is ultimately compulsory and success is desirable for all) is a quasi-market in which not all consumers are presented with any real choice; the third that there is no conclusive evidence of marketization delivering added value in terms of school improvement.[9]

Despite these objections, the language of the market has dominated the debate about schooling in England and many other countries since the 1980s. Furthermore, it can be argued that these objections concern largely the implementation of markets in education rather than the less problematic notion that education is subject to market forces in the broadest sense. Fundamentally, a market is a means of procuring desired goods and services

---

[7] Existentialism, as developed by Sartre, posits that human consciousness constitutes the self as both subject and nothingness. One can either live in 'bad faith' by pretending to be object, rather than subject, or create meaningful identity through one's choices, responsibilities and commitments. In a sense, Giddens' arguments in *Modernity and Self Identity* and elsewhere amount to a claim that this need to combat existential nothingness is exacerbated by social and cultural changes that make society increasingly individualized and reflexive.

[8] See, for example, James Tooley's response to the work of Christopher Winch: Tooley, J. (1998) 'The Neo-Liberal Critique of State Intervention in Education: a reply to Winch', *Journal of Philosophy of Education* 32/2, 267–282; Winch, C. (1996) *Quality and Education*, Oxford: Blackwell.

[9] For a summary of the critiques, with a particular focus on the third, see Lauder, H. and Hughes, D. (1999) *Trading in Futures: why markets in education don't work*, Buckingham: Open University Press. Much of the literature, however, is less clear-cut on whether or not there are measurable benefits of marketization. For an alternative, and perhaps less politically committed, view to Lauder and Hughes, see the work of Stephen Gorard, e.g. Gorard, S. and Taylor, C. (2001) *A Preliminary Consideration of the Impact of Market Forces on Educational Standards*, Cardiff: Cardiff University School of Social Sciences.

through trade. At the most minimal of levels, therefore, every school system can be seen in market terms, given that funding is allocated (either by the individual, or collectively) to provide a desired service. Furthermore, funding allocated to education is dependent on what a society feels it can and should afford, and therefore on the success of markets in other goods and services. If we accept this, the two objections above become arguments about the status, functioning and efficiency of educational markets, rather than about whether education is, or can avoid being, subject to market forces.

It is not the purpose of the present chapter to debate the functioning of educational markets, though an extensive literature exists on this. However, the market metaphor will be adopted here, according to the minimal argument above, but with the still relatively unusual purpose, at least, at the school level, of examining the role of the student as active agent within that market.[10]

In a large two-volume work by Clune and Witte on educational markets in the USA, there is no reference whatever to students as choosers.[11] The debate has been framed almost exclusively in terms of school as producer, parent as consumer and child as product. Clearly the assumption of parents as consumers has some economic logic, insofar as parents, *en bloc*, could be said to be funding education, though the degree to which they can exercise individual choice in this matter is highly limited for all but the most wealthy. However, this formulation also assumes a very traditional transmission model of education, which ignores the constructivist learning theory which has dominated the psychology of education for several decades. According to these non-constructivist assumptions, knowledge is absolute, and resides in the institution, which dispenses it into the empty vessels we call students to the satisfaction, or not, of parents who exercise limited rights to choose between dispensers. It is essentially a Fordist, production-line view of schooling with the schooled student as the end product.

Learning theorists long ago rejected such a view. (It is over a century since John Dewey published *My Pedagogic Creed*.[12]) According to all shades of constructivist learning theory, the learner actively constructs knowledge, subjectively and intersubjectively, on the basis of previous understanding and experience. Even a traditional education, focusing on

---

[10] There has been much more attention to the student as prime mover within further and higher education. For example, in 2002, WorldCat (the World Catalogue of books) listed over 500 titles under the heading of 'student choice'.

[11] Clune,W.H. and Witte, J.F. (1990) *Choice and Control in American Education*, New York: Falmer.

[12] 'My Pedagogic Creed', in Dworkin, M.S. (ed.) (1959) *Dewey on Education: a selection*, New York: Teachers College Press. Dewey is generally seen as pre-dating the development of constructivism *per se*, but is clearly influential in the development of such thinking.

cultural heritage, does not pass on fixed conceptions of heritage from one generation to the next: as evidenced, for example, by the debates in England concerning the desirable core of the history curriculum, and the list of pre-twentieth century literary works that can be said to comprise the English literary heritage.[13] John Beck, for example, has argued that a reading of cultural heritage as cultural transmission is flawed because Western 'high culture' is characterizable, principally, by a focus on critique rather than initiation into a received and immutable canon.[14] Teachers, likewise, modify knowledge in their teaching of it, as well as in their own understandings, as 'subject matter knowledge' becomes 'pedagogic content knowledge': knowledge as taught.[15]

Therefore, while it is undeniable that in one sense parents are consumers in the education market, insofar as they make choices on behalf of their children and pay taxes to fund the provision among which those choices occur, these proxy-choices do not only diminish with increasing age of the child, but are made dialogically from very early ages, in that they are made with reference to the child's interests, aptitudes, psychological and emotional development and, increasingly, express wishes.[16]

Students are involved in the choices at the macro level, such as choice of institution and choice of course, that parents make on their behalf, when such choices are offered. Perhaps more importantly, and certainly inevitably, students make their own choices about level and type of involvement, with respect to their own attitudes and motivations, at the micro level of the particular school event. That educational success or failure is dependent on orientation towards schooling has also been known for some time, and there have been high-profile studies of how groups of pupils negotiate the school experience in terms of their cultural and social identities on a minute-to-minute basis, such as Paul Willis's *Learning to Labour*.[17] Nevertheless, the view remains among many researchers that too

---

[13] Much has been written on both these issues. For example, see Robert Phillips (1998) *History Teaching, Nationhood and the State: a study in educational politics*, London: Cassell, and Section 1 (National Perspectives on Literacy Policy) of Marum, E. (ed.) (1996) *Children and Books in the Modern World: contemporary perspectives on literacy*, London: Falmer.

[14] Beck, J. (1996) Nation, Curriculum and Identity in Conservative Cultural Analysis: a critical commentary, *Cambridge Journal of Education*, 26/2, 171–198.

[15] Shulman, L. (1986) Those Who Understand: knowledge growth in teaching, *Educational Researcher* 15/2, 4–14.

[16] (Do we so easily accept that parents are the consumers of higher education? They also, and increasingly, pay for this too.)

[17] Willis, P.E. (1977) *Learning to Labour: how working class kids get working class jobs*, Farnborough: Saxon House.

much emphasis can be given to the student experience, given that this is socially and culturally determined. It can be countered that all choices are constrained, including adults', and that few would dispute that student involvement is at the very heart of the learning process.

A second argument for positioning students as products and not consumers within a market explanation of schooling is that school students are not mature adults, and therefore cannot make mature choices; by contrast, they are liable to exploitation as a result of the choices made on their behalf. This perspective calls forth discussion of two interrelated issues which will be the subjects of the next chapter: the validity of a deficit model of childhood, and the relationship of schooling to the broader social, cultural and legal frameworks in which emergent adults operate. (See particularly Chapters 3, 4 and 5.) Studies from Willis onwards have shown clearly, however, how children make very significant choices (not, perhaps, always fully conscious) in terms of their negotiation of the constraints of schooling. In the meantime, therefore, we shall pursue the implications of a view of students as consumers within the educational market, granting that consumers of education, as of every other service and product, can be misled, exploited and forced to take responsibility from positions of relative ignorance.

If the students are the consumers, how do they see the product? It is appropriate to consider at this point how much we know from the research literature of students' own perspectives on the experience of schooling, focusing on those still in compulsory schooling, i.e. those for whom institutionalization is not a matter of personal choice. There is still relatively little literature in this area. The belief that children and young adults should not have a major voice in the research literature because they cannot, almost by definition, know best, is deeply ingrained. The fact that what they know is of crucial importance, whether it is 'best' or not, is still under-recognized.

A corollary of this is that certain methodological approaches are predicated on assumptions which, of themselves, invalidate the student voice. Many of the best known studies of adolescents faced with curriculum choices for the first time, such as Peter Woods' *The Divided School*[18] and Stephen Ball's *Beachside Comprehensive*,[19] are essentially sociological studies which aim from the outset to show how individual choice can be explained in terms of institutional and societal constraints. While such research has obvious policy relevance in explaining the contexts for individual action, it runs the danger of relegating the individual student's perception and experience almost to the point of complete irrelevance. By contrast, studies which have overtly failed to address structural context to

---

[18] Woods, P. (1979) *The Divided School*, London: Routledge and Kegan Paul.
[19] Ball, S.J. (1981) *Beachside Comprehensive: a case study of secondary schooling*, Cambridge: Cambridge University Press.

such a degree, yet have valorized instead the voices of the students themselves, have concluded that students as young as 13 and 14 do make real choices.[20] Alison Kelly, for example, concluded a paper describing the *Girls Into Science and Technology* (GIST) project of the mid 1980s in England with the expressed belief that 'children's futures are... constructed... by the children themselves'.[21] To a large degree, such conclusions are implicit in prior methodological assumptions, given the enduringly problematic nature of freedom of choice from a purely philosophical perspective.

The literature that does take the student voice seriously can be grouped under three broad headings: the social experience of schooling; student self-identity in the school context; and student perspectives on the curriculum and on related matters, such as subject choice.

The literature in the first of these areas is fairly extensive and much of it predates work under the other two headings. Central to the most influential work of the 1960s, '70s and '80s, much of it undertaken in the British context, is that social class allegiance, modified by effects of gender and of school success, leads to certain kinds of implicit contract between the school and its various pupil constituencies. Given the enduring concern about the performance of average and below-average students in British schools, most of this work has tended to focus on working-class and/or disaffected pupils, though not always drawing the same conclusions. While both Willis (1977) and Brown (1987)[22] found cultural norms operating in working-class students' orientations to schooling, Brown generally sees these as more institutionally constructive and less antagonistic than does Willis, who found that many pupils were effectively negotiating strategies for avoiding schoolwork altogether.[23] Interestingly, Brown was beginning to see working-class compliance with school declining in the context of the new vocationalism of the 1980s. More recent work (see below) indicates that in the 1990s such students' adherence to traditional working-class aspirations was also disappearing, in the context of a much more fragmented and unpredictable labour market, though this should not be taken as an

---

[20] While sometimes running the risk of lack of theoretical depth.

[21] Kelly, A. (1988) Option Choice for Boys and Girls, *Research in Science and Technological Education* 6/1, 5–23. Quotation from p. 22.

[22] Brown, P. (1987) *Schooling Ordinary Kids: inequality, unemployment and the new vocationalism*, London: Tavistock.

[23] Willis, 1977, p. 28: the 'lads' are characterized by 'self-direction and thwarting of formal organisational aims'.

indication that underprivileged and underachieving students are more at ease with school cultures.[24]

Andrew Pollard's work, with various collaborators, has explored student self-identity in the school context, and is worthy of note for two reasons here: firstly, it covers the period of the Conservative reforms of the 1980s and '90s, and secondly, it takes as its primary unit of analysis the activity of the classroom, and considers a social and academic cross-section of young children in terms of their relations to this.

Among Pollard's earlier findings is that which forms the central element of his 1985 study: that pupils can broadly be understood as belonging to one of three groups in terms of classroom interaction, which the authors term 'Goodies', 'Jokers' and 'Gangs'.[25] 'Good' groups tend to be acquiescent, conscientious and unquestioning, and unwilling to act against school and authority norms. They comprise pupils of mixed social class and ability. Gang groups, by contrast, comprise the disaffected, aggressively working-class pupils, for whom school offers little reward or promise. Perhaps counter-intuitively, it is the Joker groups, comprising predominantly more able children, who succeed best at school, because they (alone) effectively negotiate the business of the classroom with the teacher by challenging authority in various ways while remaining essentially committed to individual and school success. Essentially, the 'Jokers' make something of the classroom for themselves by engaging critically with it; though they may not be the easiest pupils for teachers to deal with, they are ultimately the most rewarding. While Pollard and collaborators' later case studies of younger children in the 1980s and '90s are significant in showing how social and curriculum factors interact in constructing the individual child's school experience, the study of how Joker groups effectively construct the classroom experience is perhaps most obviously germane to our consideration of pupils, rather than merely parents, as educational consumers; indeed, the role of active and committed students in the classroom could more accurately be described as lying halfway between that of consumer and co-producer of the educational experience.

There is currently a surprising dearth of literature on the life of the classroom in relation to these issues, despite the wealth of work on broader

---

[24] For example, a North American study pinpoints issues of power and resistance as key to low-achieving high school pupils' experience: Lee, P.W. (1999) 'In Their Own Voices: an ethnographic study of low-achieving students within the context of school reform', *Urban Education* 34/2, 214–244. Much of the work of the sociologist of education, Basil Bernstein, served to show how school cultures tend to be geared to the needs of the middle class, even when middle class values are inclusive, liberal and child-centred. (See Note 26.)

[25] Pollard, A. (1985) *The Social World of the Primary School*, London: Cassell.

influences on the development of personal identity, with schooling acknowledged as one such influence, though often only in the broadest sense. Classroom organization at the policy level (mixed-ability vs. setting) has, of course, been considered. However, in terms of the specifics of classroom interaction, there is little that moves beyond the influential work either of Bernstein in the 1970s on framing and classification or the essentially socially-critical assumption that small-group collaborative work empowers,[26] despite a wealth of publications taking a sociocultural perspective on classroom language.[27] Pollard and Filer's later work is probably the most extensive available to date, exploring the development of self-identity as a learner on the basis of a series of longitudinal case studies. In *The Social World of Pupil Career* (1999),[28] they define four 'dimensions of strategic action' as Conformity, Re-Definition, Non-Conformity and Anti-Conformity, with Non-Conformity relating to confident manipulation of classroom norms in the style of the Joker. By contrast, in both the Conformity and Anti-Conformity states, the student plays little constructive part in the development of classroom dialogue.

Pollard and Filer's work shows how a variety of contextual factors, within and beyond the school, impact on students' classroom behaviour, broadly understood, and the extent to which there is variation among the student body in terms of the roles students play in shaping classroom experience. What is of particular note here is that those who are most active in this respect are often also most successful.

Jean Rudduck, Roland Chaplain and Gwen Wallace's work on the potential role of students in school improvement has been influential. In a context of social breakdown and fragmentation, they argue that the need to understand the student context and experience is magnified. Ironically, however, these young people have traditionally been excluded from the consultative process when it comes to the management of schools. This, claim the authors, 'is founded upon an outdated view of childhood which fails to acknowledge children's capacity to reflect on issues affecting their

---

[26] Bernstein, B. (1975) *Class and Pedagogies: visible and invisible*, Paris: OECD; Young, R. (1992) *Critical Theory and Classroom Talk*, Clevedon: Multilingual Matters.

[27] One of the key movers in this field is Neil Mercer: see, for example (2000) *Words and Minds: how we use language to think together*, London: Routledge. Such literature deals extensively with student collaboration and group work, but only addresses the issue of empowerment and the development of different classroom identities, as discussed here, implicitly.

[28] Pollard, A. and Filer, A. (1999) *The Social World of Pupil Career: strategic biographies through primary school*, London: Cassell.

lives'.[29] This implies that a sensitivity to issues of developing self-identity is crucial to the development of an effective school.

Rudduck, Chaplain and Wallace's project was broad in scope, dealing with issues of primary-secondary transition, the meaning of 'working hard in school', teacher-student relations, homework, strategies of disengagement and self-worth protection (particularly among boys), stress at school, coping with examinations, and the transition from education to work. Their major findings included students' appreciation of teachers who engage in real dialogue, the importance of seeing coherence in the curriculum, and, above all, the importance of learner self-esteem. Repeatedly we learn of students whose views of themselves as learners, constructed from experiences many years prior, have impeded in the later secondary years, in terms both of attitude and outcome.

Research into student perspectives on, and experiences of, curriculum subjects, and into related issues such as subject choice and career aspiration, is still surprisingly limited, given the almost universal acceptance of constructivist perspectives on learning. In terms of student responses to individual subjects, we can briefly summarise recent research in England with 13–15 year-olds under two headings: subject preference and perception of subject importance. There is, however, only limited correlation between these.[30]

In the late 1990s, in a study sponsored by the Economic and Social Research Council in England,[31] subject preference continued to show a degree of variation by gender, by school and by age of student, with some volatility in subject preference even between ages 14 and 15. The researchers were able to compare subject preferences and perceptions of subject importance in 1984/5 and 1996/7. The sporadic attempts to research these in Britain reveal some enduring broad patterns, at least since the 1970s: notably, a relative dislike of modern foreign languages, music and religious education. In 1996, National Curriculum implementation in

---

[29] Rudduck, J., Chaplain, R. and Wallace, G. (eds) (1996) *School Improvement: what can pupils tell us?* London: David Fulton. Quotation from p.172.

[30] There is evidence of a broader connection between personal interests and subject choices, however, such choices do not appear arbitrary: Elsworth, G.R., Harvey-Beavis, A., Ainley, J. and Fabris, S. (1999) 'Generic Interests and School Subject Choice', *Educational Research and Evaluation* 5/3, 290–318.

[31] Stables, A. and Wikeley, F. (1997) Changes in Preference for, and Perception of Relative Importance of, Subjects During a Period of Educational Reform. *Educational Studies* 23/3, 393–403; Wikeley, F. and Stables, A. (1999) 'Changes in School Students' Approaches to Subject Option Choices: a study of pupils in the West of England in 1984 and 1996', *Educational Research* 41/3, 287–299. This project provides the findings described on pages 19–20.

England and Wales seemed to have had only limited effect on patterns of relative subject preference (though the only non-National Curriculum subject commonly taken at this age – drama – increased in popularity dramatically since 1984 relative to the other subjects, while there was a fall in the position of its sister subject, English, despite its position as a National Curriculum core subject).

The lack of correlation between subject preference and perception of subject importance can be seen particularly clearly in the case of the creative arts: art and drama were both widely enjoyed in 1984/5 and 1996/7 but were credited with little importance in both studies. Music, however, was neither strongly enjoyed nor found important in school in the mid-1990s. Games and physical education were highly rated for enjoyment, yet not considered important as subjects. Very few students of this age, however, appear to respond to the content and processes of school subjects as leading to personal development on a number of fronts. Creative satisfaction, such as might be gained from art, is of secondary importance.

Reasons for subject preference are difficult to explore without extensive interviews with large numbers of students. However, perceived ability is clearly an important factor in subject preference whilst the role of the individual teacher is more difficult to determine. In general, students are attracted to subject processes rather than subject content; this applies particularly to boys.

Perception of subject importance, by contrast, seems very stable across time, school and gender. Students see strong utilitarian value in mathematics, English and science and credit these with overriding importance. National Curriculum implementation in England and Wales seems only to have reinforced this tendency. Meanwhile, creative arts subjects and religious education tend to be seen as relatively unimportant, and the importance of music in popular culture is by no means reflected in its importance rating as a school subject, where perceived career usefulness is of paramount concern. Similarly, art and drama were not seen as important in either 1984/5 or 1996/7, despite being well liked.

In contrast to subject preference, perceived ability seems to play only a limited part in perception of subject importance: particularly in mathematics, motivation is largely extrinsic and instrumental.

Underplaying the importance of their own abilities and interests when assessing subject importance may have a negative effect on students' career choices in the longer term, particularly if they regard the employment market as a stable 'given' rather than concentrate in a more general way on the development of their own skills. Furthermore, the naive linkage of school subjects to careers ('there's no point in doing Art unless you're going to be an artist') not only betrays a narrow view of education but is also potentially problematic in its assumptions. Overall, what emerges is a largely instrumental view of the curriculum (in the narrow, vernacular rather than Deweyan sense) which, on the one hand, acknowledges the abiding importance of qualifications in mathematics, English and science for a wide range of careers while drawing, on the other hand, direct and concrete links between other subjects and careers which are naive. There appears to be little sophistication in students' thinking about the use of school subjects. They do not tend to refer to subjects as useful because of the skills or habits of mind they engender, but rather because they might be 'needed' to help secure a good job. Thus their motivations, at least with regard to perceptions of subject importance, seem almost entirely extrinsic and either very general ('you need maths whatever you want to do') or unrealistically specific ('There's no point in doing RE unless you want to be a vicar'; 'I don't need French because I'm not going to work abroad').[32]

The Stables and Wikeley project has implications for our present focus on the student as the prime consumer of education in a context of increasingly individualized risk-taking. The current labour market has little to offer for those with high ambitions but few or no marketable skills such as must be gained through commitment, motivation and directed choice. It seems clear that careers advice which focuses on clarifying pupils' ambitions, without realistic assessment of the steps necessary (and feasible) for the individuals in pursuit of those ambitions, renders it too easy for pupils in schools to fail to come to terms with the complexities of the labour market, its relationship with schooling, and the very indirect linkage of school subjects to occupational and professional activity. Pupils may also be deeply unaware of the varying degrees of competition pertaining to entry to different careers.

It seems likely that many students will fail in their aspirations, through a lack of cultural and social capital. A hypothetical example involves two students who wish to become veterinary surgeons. Student A is from a working class home where no parents or close relatives have experienced higher education; student B has graduate parents and is from a professional background. Student B's aspirations are likely to be tempered from the first by the knowledge that success in A level sciences will not be sufficient to gain access to a relevant degree course; his parents and others will have stressed that veterinary science is so popular that Grades A and B at A2 level are almost certain to be required.[33] If student A is only aware that it is necessary to be 'good at science', he or she may well persist for longer in

---

[32] See Stables and Wikeley, 1997; Wikeley and Stables, 1999.

[33] A2 levels have replaced the traditional British A (=Advanced) Level examination, taken usually at age 18. Students now take a series of AS (Advanced Supplementary) examinations at age 17, and specialize in (usually) three subjects at A2 level. AS, as well as A2, marks can count towards the final A Level grade. Passing Grades are A-E.

pursuit of an unrealisable aim rather than making more realistic plans for the future. With recent changes in the labour market in increasingly technologized societies resulting in the removal of many forms of post-16 on-the-job training, more students are inevitably placed in situations requiring largely academic qualifications (i.e. those including significant amounts of writing and book-learning), yet only a proportion come from backgrounds that prepare them for this Although existing research is of insufficient scope to give a detailed account of the extent of this problem, the inevitable absence of knowledgeable support from the home for many students facing a changing labour market renders the task of teachers and careers advisors even more critical than formerly in preparing pupils to make career choices which are likely to prove fruitful.

Schools, therefore, have an educational duty to help students make choices. After all, risk, like stress, can be productive or inhibiting: threat or opportunity. Andrew Pollard, for example, notes that poorly managed classrooms increase risk as threat, whereas established classroom routines allow pupils to engage in more risk-taking as opportunity.[34] The move towards greater individualization of risk does not, therefore, imply an educational response which removes supporting structures but rather one which reinforces them, provided that the structures in question really do support rather than inhibit. As Berger and Luckmann discussed in some depth in the 1960s, a degree of empowerment over objective structures arises from purposeful intersubjective activity;[35] in that sense, the quality of the social experience of schooling is central to the development of the networking and risk-taking, as opposed to merely socialized, individual.

Any consideration of the response of educators to the individualization of risk, however, supposes a set of assumptions about childhood. It is important, therefore, to consider the nature of childhood itself, and this will be the focus of the next chapter. If children are merely incomplete dependents, they should be sheltered from significant exposure to risk. If, however, the difference between child and adult is more one of relative experience, a different perspective emerges.

---

[34] Pollard, 1985 (Note 25). Pollard argues that classroom management strategies exist to promote meaningful interaction, and thus, in the best cases, to impact positively on learner self-identity.

[35] Berger, P.L. and Luckmann, T. (1966) *The Social Construction of Reality: a treaty in the sociology of knowledge*, New York: Irvington.

Chapter 3

Diverse Experience; Diverse Childhoods

Ideas about education are inextricably linked to ideas about childhood, and individualization theses also inevitably concern children. Views of childhood are subject to considerable historical variation. In recent years, both Romantic ideals and psychological deficit views of childhood have been open to challenge. Any changes of belief about the specialness of childhood can have significant effects for educational policy and practice.

There are strong, potentially conflicting, strands in views of childhood since the Enlightenment. The assumption of children as fallen is part of the Christian tradition, and fallen children must have their wilfulness suppressed. At the same time, there is also a strong tradition, owing a good deal to Plato and reinforced by Romanticism, of the idealization of childhood.[1] The assumption of children as incomplete, or unformed, is, of course, much more broadly held and underpins assumptions about schooling and formal education beyond the Christian and Western worlds. However, while children (young children, at least) clearly are dependent on adults, students of childhood are less inclined now towards 'deficit' explanations of the child than was the case in the middle years of the twentieth century.[2] Furthermore, the social context of childhood has changed in late, or post modernity. Jenks writes: 'Individuals are now much more recognizable through their immediate location and project than through their group affiliations or previously established identity',[3] and this lack of unquestioned belonging can make children more prone to mental and physical abuse than hitherto. Thus for reasons both psychological and

---

[1] Good general texts on the history of childhood include Jenks, C. (1996) *Childhood*, London: Routledge; DeMause, L. (ed.) (1976) *The History of Childhood*, London: Souvenir Press; Hoyles, M. (ed.) (1979) *Changing Childhood*, London: Writers and Readers Publishing Co-operative.

[2] For example, see Bruner, J. and Haste, H. (eds) (1987) *Making Sense: the child's construction of the world*, London: Methuen. This collection of articles concerns the primacy of the social (particularly language) in developing the cognitive, such that development is not 'the growth of autonomous cognitive structures' as implied by the work of Piaget and others.

[3] Jenks, 1996, p.102.

sociological, some of the most basic assumptions about childhood, and, therefore, about education and schooling have been problematized. This chapter will consider the key approaches to childhood vis-a-vis education in the twentieth century, and show how each can be subject to fundamental critique. To this end, two common conceptions of the child are identified: the Wordsworthian Romantic conception of the child, and the deficiency model. All in all, we have tended to exaggerate the specialness of childhood, and the differences between children and adults, seeing children simultaneously as 'trailing clouds of glory'[4] and as incapable of higher mental processes and moral judgment.

'Trailing clouds of glory': the Wordsworthian/Romantic Conception of the Child

The neo-Platonic notion of the child as apprehender of ideal forms, subject to corruption by the socializing influence of adults, may sit uneasily with the Christian orthodoxy of the Fall from Grace, but none the less has exerted a potent influence on educational thought since the Enlightenment. Such a notion is perhaps most commonly associated with two names in Western educational thought: the philosopher Jean-Jacques Rousseau and the poet William Wordsworth.

Rousseau's *Émile* remains a profoundly influential work, though, as Allan Bloom reminds us, it was never intended as a simple teaching manual.[5] Indeed, some ideas strongly associated with twentieth century thought can be traced to him, such as the sublimation of sexual desire, collaboration as a product of the 'selfish gene', the dietary benefits of fresh vegetables and the desirability of mothers breast-feeding their own children. He marks, perhaps more strongly than any other individual, the transition in Eighteenth Century thought from the 'Age of Reason' to pre-eminent belief in feeling and soul. He was thus a strong influence not only on Romantics such as Wordsworth, but on others including Kant and Nietzsche. Rousseau saw himself as an heir to Plato, and *Émile* deserves serious consideration as the finest work in the philosophy of education since Plato's *Republic*.[6]

Émile can be regarded as the first, and perhaps still the most compelling, argument for child-centred, 'progressive' education, although it runs counter to many of the socializing tendencies of more recent writings in this area (including those of John Dewey, who may well be seen as North

---

4   William Wordsworth: *Ode: Intimations of Immortality*, in Hutchinson, T. (ed.) (revised Selincourt, E.) (1973) *Wordsworth: Poetical Works*, Oxford: Oxford University Press, pp. 460–462.

5   Rousseau, J-J., ed. Bloom, A. (1979) *Émile, or On Education*, New York: Basic.

6   Ed., Lee, D. (1974) London: Penguin.

America's foremost 'child of Rousseau'[7]). Rousseau finds in the child a natural self-interest which should be left to develop, acting through the active principle of growth, until the adult, from a position of strong self-knowledge, learns to bestow kindness on those less fortunate and to form social contracts (notably in marriage) out of mutual self-interest. Unlike other Enlightenment contract theorists (Locke, and, particularly, Hobbes), Rousseau abhors the notion of social contracts derived from fear and weakness, seeing these as the property of a bourgeois public sphere that inhibits natural growth. Indeed, his championing of the natural is so eloquent that in many respects the opening of Book 1 of *Émile* seems valid as a rallying cry for environmentalists at the millennium:

'Everything...degenerates in the hands of man. He forces one soil to nourish the products of another, one tree to bear the fruit of another. He mixes and confuses the climates, the elements, the seasons.'

It is easy to forget, however, that this is also a profoundly conservative philosophy in some senses. It is certainly opposed to social welfare. For example, there is every reason to think that Rousseau would have abhorred the increasing State interference in education that has characterized the last Century and a half. Despite the valorization of self-interest, Rousseau realized that the child needs help from adults; he also realized that children who had been so helped would learn, naturally, to respect the helping adults. In opposition to, say, Dewey, however, Rousseau was clear that children do not need to be socialized. He shared the belief of many of the founding fathers of modern liberalism that the individual could act as an autonomous rational agent, though 'rational' in this case implies sensibility and not mere 'reason'. What they need is knowledge of the realities and necessities of life: in the original sense, 'natural science'. What he felt they did *not* need was training in the dominant discourses of philosophy and social life, and it is there that late modern and postmodern thinking so radically departs from him.

While Rousseau's influence on education world-wide may be immense, William Wordsworth's evocation of his own childhood in *The Prelude* is perhaps more consciously evoked as an influence on educational practice in Britain[8] – though his influence on American writers such as Whitman, Emerson and Thoreau, whose work has had far-reaching implications for all aspects of North American culture, may also have been strong. Widely accepted as the father of English Romanticism, Wordsworth echoed many

---

[7]　For an overview, see Dworkin, M.S. (ed.) (1959) *Dewey on Education: a selection*, New York: Teachers College Press.

[8]　In Hutchinson (ed.) (Note 4) pp. 495–588.

beliefs of Rousseau's in his championing of an essentially apolitical, anti-urban, nature-worshipping, solitary educational ethic. Wordsworth echoes Rousseau in stating that 'the child is father of the man' and that we are born 'trailing clouds of glory'.[9]

Wordsworth's influence is invoked directly by Marjorie Hourd, whose *The Education of the Poetic Spirit*, published in 1949, was one of the first major works of English education written by a university-based academic educationalist and teacher-trainer in the UK.[10] Hourd prefaces her work with two extracts from *The Prelude*. Though on one level, Hourd's argument is simply that education should be child-centred, and she refers to work in child psychology to support this, there is a real sense too of a belief in *revealing*, and not simply moulding, the self of the child through creative activity: she states, for example, that 'Who am I?' is the first 'important question' asked in early childhood (p. 23), though the question develops in sophistication as the child matures. In the assertion, 'I am not suggesting that after that the child thoroughly understands his own personality, for this is a life-time pursuit' (p. 23), there is the implication of a given essence of personality reminiscent of Wordsworth's belief that 'not in complete forgetfulness... but trailing clouds of glory do we come, from God who is our home'.[11] The Wordsworthian child inherits the power of Imagination (as Wordsworth defined it, 'Seeing into the life of things'[12]), and it is principally through the use of the imagination that Hourd, and her successors, felt that education would lead to personal growth.

This essentially Romantic vision dominated educational thinking in the schools context in Britain in the 1960s, bolstered by the early findings of child psychologists such as Susan Isaacs and Ruth Griffiths[13] that children really do learn through play. It has remained an extremely powerful element in teacher thinking since, despite (in the field of the language arts) the increasing concern of professional writers such as those connected with the so-called 'Movement' in the 1950s and beyond with the conscious use of form in creative composition, and the increasingly culturally materialist

---

[9] Ode: Intimations of Immortality.

[10] Hourd, M. (1949) *The Education of the Poetic Spirit*, London: Heinemann.

[11] Ode: Intimations of Immortality.

[12] *Lines: written above Tintern Abbey*, in Hutchinson, ed., pp.163–165.

[13] Griffiths, R. (1938) *Imagination and Play in Childhood*, London: University of London Institute of Education and the Home and School Council of Great Britain; Isaacs, S. (1930) *Intellectual Growth in Young Children*, and (1933) *Social Development in Young Children*, both London: Routledge and Kegan Paul.

tendency in literary-critical studies in universities which has done all that it can in recent decades to destroy the myth of the Romantic ego, even of the unified subject.[14] Oblivious, it would seem, to influences around it, the myth of the supernatural child, whose growth will come from self-expression, has remained a powerful force in schooling throughout the latter decades of the twentieth century. Certainly, research on English teachers in the UK in the 1990s by Goodwyn and Findlay showed most to be committed to a 'personal growth', as opposed to a 'cultural analysis', 'cultural heritage', 'adult needs' or 'cross-curricular' approach to their subject.[15] There is still a widespread belief among teachers, for example, that children must be allowed to 'express themselves' in writing prior to, rather than after, formal training in the rhetoric and genres of written language.

Piagetian Constructivism and Stage Theories: the Deficit Model of the Child

An emphasis on the *a priori* knowledge or worth of the child does not sit easily with constructivist theories of learning. At face value, it would seem that a child-centred philosophy must concentrate on how the child builds his or her own understanding of the world; in fact, constructivism rests on the assumption that the neonate knows nothing. To the constructivist, knowledge comes with experience, albeit Piagetian stage theory assumes cognitive readiness precedes any specific learning. Despite Noam Chomsky's linking of an innate capacity to learn language with an explanation of cultural influence,[16] to many twentieth century constructivists, however, another truth is evident: that the child *cannot* learn what the adult can learn; that the child's cognitive apparatus is incomplete. To Rousseau and Wordsworth, the child was often more than the adult; to Piaget (and, by implication, to Vygotsky

---

[14] For a general history of trends in literary criticism, from a Marxist perspective, see Terry Eagleton (1983) *Literary Theory: an introduction*, Oxford: Blackwell; for a specific introduction to cultural materialism, John Brannigan (1998) *New Historicism and Cultural Materialism*, Basingstoke: Macmillan; for a counter-attack on anti-liberal humanist perspectives, Harold Bloom (1995) *The Western Canon*, Basingstoke: Macmillan and (1998) *Shakespeare: the invention of the human*, New York: Riverhead.

[15] Goodwyn, A. and Findlay, K. (1999) 'The Cox Models Revisited: English teachers' views of their subject and the National Curriculum' *English in Education* 33/2, 19–31. The five approaches to English teaching cited here originate from 'The Cox Report': Department for Education and Science (UK) (1989) *English for Ages 5 to 16*, London: HMSO.

[16] For a general introduction to Chomsky, see Lyons, J. (1977) *Chomsky*, London: Fontana.

and to others), the child was most certainly less.[17] Chomsky, for all his influence on linguistics, is less of a seminal figure with regard to pedagogy and curriculum. Piaget, particularly, is responsible for instilling notions such as that the pre-adolescent child is incapable of abstract thought or 'formal operations'. While Piaget's research, conducted with very small samples under laboratory conditions, has certainly drawn educators' attention to the fact that children *develop* in terms of their learning, it has now been shown by a number of commentators to have been simplistic and over-normative in its accounts of how that development takes place. Specifically, children are capable of many kinds of thinking Piaget thought them incapable of, given the appropriate social conditions.[18] At its worst, Piaget's legacy has justified, even valorized, the essentially lazy teaching practice of explaining that a child who, for example, is not concentrating on his or her work is 'not yet ready' for that work and will get round to being ready for it in his or her own time. Piagetian thinking has also resulted in strict age groupings in schools and has helped to justify standardization of the curriculum.

At the Millennium, it may be that a less dramatic view than either of the above is re-emerging: that the child, particularly the older child, is simply less experienced than the adult. The emphasis on learning has shifted from that of the individual mind gradually making sense of the world to one of learning through socially mediated experience.[19] This is not to deny that there is no validity at all in stage theory: research into language development, for instance, continues to show that certain kinds of growth dependent on exposure to language must occur during critical periods, or that capacity to develop language fully is lost.[20] This is a much less prescriptive formulation, however, and, educationally, it is enabling rather than disabling, since it encourages unrestricted exposure to language for

---

[17] Vygotsky was one of the first to question Piaget. Nevertheless, they seemed to share certain assumptions. (See Chapter 1, Note 19.)

[18] Paul Light, in Bruner and Haste (Note 2) (Chapter 2, Taking Roles, pp. 41–61) discusses how children are capable of certain operations that Piaget found them incapable of when these are presented in personally meaningful contexts; he cites Piaget and Inhelder's 'Three Mountains' experiment, that purports to show (wrongly, in his view) that young children cannot take another's perspective. See also Margaret Donaldson (1978) *Children's Minds*, London: Fontana.

[19] For a social psychological perspective, Bruner and Haste (1987 – above); for an explicitly discursive account of meaning making, Edwards, D. and Potter, J. (1992) *Discursive Psychology*, London: Sage; for a sociocultural and discursive perspective on learning in the classroom context, Mercer, N. (2000) *Words and Minds*, London: Routledge.

[20] See, for example, Lipsitt, L.P. and Reese, H.W. (1978) *Child Development*, London: Scott Foresman and Co., pp. 33–34.

everyone throughout life. Piagetian stage theory, by contrast, can effectively restrict the child's capacity to learn by assuming that it does not exist.

This is more a re-emergent than an emergent view in that it is in some respects essentially the view of childhood that was emerging in Western thought prior to Rousseau and Romanticism (when, following disillusion by some with the corrupt urbanity and complacency of the most committed disciples of the Age of Reason, a mythical view of childhood took hold). In the *Essay on Human Understanding*, which might be seen as a seminal text of constructivism, Locke constructed, at the end of the seventeenth century, an account of human knowledge which needs no support from either extreme view of the child, yet which has been used by many since as a justification for values of liberal tolerance, mutual respect and civic order.[21] In Locke's view, knowledge is dependent on both sensory experience and socially shared 'ideas'. Although Locke was an archetypal late seventeenth, early eighteenth century liberal, his view of the individual mind did not lapse into solipsism. Also, while he urged that those with children in their care try to see the world through a child's eyes, he did not argue that children were restricted in their capacity to learn.[22] The Lockean view steers a course between the two later extremes of idealization of the child and the deficiency model, while rejecting the earlier, cruder formulations of children as merely the untutored inheritors of original sin (though little account was to be taken of any incapacity to learn on this assumption).

A little later, Kant further developed a view of human understanding through his three great *Critiques* (of Pure Reason, Practical Reason and Judgement). The Kantian view is that human knowledge and understanding are socially constructed insofar as sensory input is organized in terms of pre-existing Categories; however, it remains realist, in epistemological terms, as Kant believed in the concreteness of physical matter, and also that experience has the power to cause redefinition of Categories, for example via experiences of the sublime.[23]

In very broad terms, more recent learning theories take us back to such less dramatic conceptions of childhood than those inherited from Romanticism and the early twentieth century (albeit that in some other respects, we would now find many ancient child-rearing practices repellant[24]). While the capacity to learn may be inbred, learning seems to

---

[21] *Essay Concerning Human Understanding*, ed. Nidditch, P.H. (1975) Oxford: Oxford University Press.

[22] *Some Thoughts Concerning Education*, ed. Yolton, J.W. (2000) Oxford: Oxford University Press.

[23] Guyer, P. (ed.) (1992) *The Cambridge Companion to Kant*, Cambridge: Cambridge University Press.

[24] See, for example, contributions to DeMause (1976) (Note 1 above).

depend both on individual sensory experience and on engagement with socially constructed norms and classifications, yet there is no justification for an over-emphasis on pre-determined educational 'stages', since the nature of learning is fundamentally the same for all people at all times, albeit that motivations, and even capacities, are not constant. We may be less inclined to a belief in God-given Reason than our eighteenth-century forebears, but in many respects the rationalist-empiricist synthesis offered, to very varying degrees of sophistication, by both Locke and Kant, bequeaths us a view of the child as both eminently teachable and eminently worthy to be taught. Recent research in neuroscience tends to reinforce this essentially optimistic view, showing how the brain responds quickly and effectively to new stimuli, and how emotional response can facilitate cognitive growth.[25]

Overall, then, we have inherited a set of assumptions about childhood, many of which are now problematic. This encourages an increased skepticism towards both the idealized view of the child, inherited from Plato, Rousseau and Wordsworth, and the deficit model of childhood associated most strongly with Piaget. Educators following this line no longer regard features such as intelligence as immutable, so that you can 'show me the child and I'll show you the man' nor regard children as predestined for specific spheres or strata of society. Children are neither angels nor fallen angels nor devils. They are neither necessarily wiser nor stupider than adults, except insofar as they have less experience.

Yet childhood remains qualitatively different from adulthood in other, less problematized respects. Children are less aware of (some of) the ways of the world, and in that sense remain vulnerable and needing adult protection. By the same token, adults feel they need protection against the consequences of the inexperience and sometimes the energy, of youth; hence our denial of the vote, or of alcohol, to those under eighteen. Young children are also physically vulnerable. Children are less responsible than adults, in both senses of the world. Children undergo physical changes associated with growth, and physical and emotional issues are associated with this. Also, as noted above, stage theory, while discredited in its more rigid formulations, is not completely without foundation: children both tend to behave and think in certain ways at certain ages, and can pass through critical periods for certain kinds of learning.

We hope, of course, that childhood will be magical, but we wish that for adults, too. We know that children play – but perhaps by characterizing childish activity as play we are often simply dismissing its usefulness to us

---

[25] For application of such insights into classroom practice, see Kovalik, S. and Olsen, K. (2001) *Exceeding Expectations: a user's guide to implementing brain research in the classroom*, Covington, WA: Books for Educators.

as adults, whose most satisfying 'work' activities also have an element of play about them. Children take their own activities seriously, just as adults do, though children do not get paid or pay bills. Insofar as we are all equal, we are all equally part of the world: after early infancy, we are all, if we are lucky enough, salient and reflexive beings, albeit our conceptions of fairness and the like at first seem egocentric as a result of our limited experience, and our range of reference is limited.

In many ways, however, contemporary social structures ascribe and attest to a far greater sense of childhood separateness than this. On one hand we still tend to see knowledge in a number of areas as essentially corrupting for children. (This is a different argument from that which states that children *can* be corrupted by certain kinds of exposure, under certain conditions.) On the other hand, children often remain unpunished by the law for destructive behaviour, on the grounds that they are not old enough to know what they are doing – an approach, which has disturbing, effects on some communities.

What is left for education if some of these assumptions about childhood are abandoned or, at least, loosened? Perhaps, ironically, an increased role. By jettisoning the notion that children are essentially 'not ready' for certain kinds of learning, and replacing it with that of children being capable of advanced forms of doing and thinking, but only with reference to a limited range of experience, we open up the possibility of more exciting, more adventurous forms of education than have previously been practised. For example, many parents and teachers are aware that children's capacity to work in multimedia, and create what Gunther Kress has referred to as 'multi-mode objects', is impressive and is often less inhibited by fear of failure and responsibility than adults.[26] Children can thus be impressive exploiters of new technologies. If children are reflective, so can be held responsible, and can engage in many adult cultural practices (though on their own terms), we put an onus on ourselves as educators to engage with them on a new level of mutual respect. At the same time, accepting that children have differing experiences implies also accepting that there will be differences in their patterns of learning.

To accept these is to acknowledge that children are made to make real choices with real consequences, taking increasing responsibility for their own life-planning as preparation for full involvement in democratic processes as adults. Viewed from this perspective, an education which 'waits until they are ready' is actually impeding development, as is one that places heavy emphasis on commonality and standardization of curricula and pedagogy. This is a liberal position, but a hard one. Children, like adults, are, in Sartre's term, existentially 'condemned to be free'. They are also

---

[26] Kress, G. (1997) *Before Writing*, London: Routledge.

condemned to be both socially constructed and different: in debt to others, yet unique. In Rom Harré's terms, they position themselves *vis-à-vis* social norms rather than being simply determined by them.[27]

In other chapters, and particularly in the final one, there will be exploration of some of the implications of this position for teachers. At this stage, I shall limit myself to sketching out three relatively uncontroversial, yet important, spheres of learning with which educational practices should address themselves: *learning to learn, learning to think* and *learning to choose*.

Learning to Learn

It would be a mistake to assume we understand the role of educational institutions and practices with respect to learning. People would certainly learn if there were no schools or universities; do such institutions enhance learning or simply channel it? Despite the lack of informed consideration of this, perhaps rather obvious, question, there remains a considerable body of knowledge about learning in general. It can probably safely be assumed that educators wish to promote learning via their practices in at least one of the two senses above.

Learning is not merely a matter of sensation, though it may depend on sensation. Learning the rules of a form of life, or language game, in Wittgensteinian terms, will not be developed purely by 'giving children lots of experiences',[28] but by giving them the right experiences from which they learn. For children to become effective lifelong learners, attentiveness is important, as is a willingness to seek, and to learn from, both new and repeated experiences. This implies more than 'Children need to be motivated'. Motivation can all-too-easily be seen as a driver of learning that one either does or does not possess, as if by magic. By contrast, motivation can be stimulated by enjoyable and rewarding experience, thus propelling successful learners into a virtuous cycle, whereby they learn ever more from their experiences. Purely sociological accounts of the learner, stressing the advantages and disadvantages of upbringing, have, in the past, overlooked the possible psychological explanations of the increasing gap between the most and least successful at school, as they have tended to overlook the equally likely psychological explanations of the differences between the

---

[27] Harré, R. (1998) *The Singular Self*, London: Sage.

[28] Wittgenstein: *Philosophical Investigations* (1968: Oxford: Blackwell). Wittgenstein spends some time differentiating between the sensation of, say, being pricked, and the experience of pain, that is culturally determined (particularly c.p.300).

many children from deprived backgrounds who do poorly in terms of education, and the few who do very well.[29]

Management theory has already embraced the importance of the management of attention.[30] Educational thinking, however, has tended to remain stuck at the point of seeing literacy and numeracy (and perhaps oracy) as the 'basics', ignoring the skills of attentiveness and ability to make connections that help drive development in these areas. While it would be a fallacy to suppose that attention can exist without any object, the ability to focus a child's energies on potentially rewarding activity is surely a mark of effective pedagogy, though it gets less attention in the literature than it might. There is surely scope for teachers to spend more time developing skills of attention and concentration.

The relationship of motivation to success at school is by no means unproblematic, however. On the one hand, the psychological literature confirms that motivation is a key factor in stimulating learning. Interestingly, the school effectiveness literature fails to confirm this. Studies have failed to show any clear relation between proxy measures for motivation, such as measures of subject preference and perceived subject importance, and increased performance in tests and examinations.[31]

There are several possible explanations for this, other than defective research design or data analysis. It is possible that syllabus and examination requirements are too reductive to capitalize fully on students' levels of motivation. It might be that what students enjoy in lessons is not that which is tested in examinations; or even what is generally thought germane to the subject. It may be that lessons that are more fun than others are also relatively easy. Whatever the reason, for teaching not to exploit motivation is surely a wasted opportunity, and may have long-term implications. Even if motivation does not guarantee short-term test success, it is much more likely to engender a desire for what has recently been termed 'lifelong learning' than classroom experience that is purely instrumental and largely disengaged. It may be that the emphasis on effective schooling has tended to focus too much on learning for the institution rather than learning in the institution. In other words, schools' and colleges' examination results have

---

[29] Milgram, N.A. and Palti, G. (1993) Psychosocial Characteristics of Resilient Children, *Journal of Research in Personality* 27/3, 207–221.

[30] E.g. Blanchard, K. and Johnson, S. (1996) *The One Minute Manager*, London: Harper Collins Business.

[31] See, for example, C.S.J. Stables' MPhil thesis (University of Bath, 2001): *Atypically Positive Perceptions of French at Ages 13 to 14*, that failed to show any correlation between subject enjoyment, perception of subject importance and subsequent success in GCSE examinations in two schools with unusually positive student views of French.

come to be seen as the measure of good education rather than as no more than rough indications of progress to date. The danger of such an approach is that it deflects attention from surely more important educational aims: specifically the development of interests, habits of mind and orientations to learning that can ensure long-term, rather than short-term involvement. The outcomes of such aims are difficult to measure in isolation, which explains, perhaps, why they are not adopted as policy aims in the age of standardization and accountability, yet can nevertheless be identifiable, just as success and happiness can be identified but not accurately measured. In the long run, a disposition towards further learning is more important than learning any particular thing, and this becomes increasingly the case as risk is individualized and the labour market demands flexibility and transferable skills.

Learning to Think

According to Giddens, Jenks and others, late modernity is increasingly self-reflexive. However, the relationship of learning to thinking remains problematic. Learning sometimes involves thinking, but clearly not always, and thinking takes various forms, not all of which can be guaranteed development simply as the result of rewarding experience. To Wittgenstein, at least in his later work, that which is true is always true in terms of a 'language game', and cannot be said fully to be true outside it. 'Language games' are verbal 'forms of life', the rules of which we learn so that we might 'go on'.[32] Thus understood, we do not think about things so much as engage in certain language games that are evidently about things but are, in fact, no more abstracted from 'reality' than other things we do. This insight, developed by, among others, the educational genre theorists of the 1980s, has helped to promote a new respect for the disciplines in education (though not in the sense of a fixed adherence to a set of 'subjects' unchanging over time), in that the content of thought can no longer be seen as separate from the processes of thinking or of doing.[33] Forms of thinking are thus forms of cultural practice.

---

[32] This idea of knowing how to go on is returned to on numerous occasions throughout the *Philosophical Investigations*.

[33] The degree to which genres penetrate and define social practices is made clear by a reading of Christie, F. and Martin, J.R. (eds) (1997) *Genre and Institutions: social processes in the workplace and school*, London: Cassell.

Learning to think, therefore, involves learning a profusion of discourses, or ways of thinking, embodied in 'communities of practice'. We can learn to think mathematically and historically, speculatively and imaginatively, analytically and analogically.[34] It seems clear that the development of such diverse forms of thinking must require exposure, understanding and practice (though Wittgenstein might question the commonly held distinction between the latter two: we need to learn 'how to go on'). Again, however, none of these will have so much effect on the child who is not in the habit of learning in the areas concerned.

Closely related to the idea of genre is that of ground rules. In *School Writing*, Douglas Barnes and Yanina Sheeran argue that much student failure comes from a mismatch between student and teacher assumptions.[35] In other words, it is not so much that teachers do not explain things clearly, as that they do not explain enough. What teachers fail to explain are the things they, as experts take for granted: the basic operating rules for the subject. Teachers, as subject experts, have 'buried' these operating rules in their subconscious minds, where they can be accessed without conscious thought (a process referred to by psychologists as 'ontic dumping'[36]). Thus it is quite natural – though less than ideal teaching – for teachers not to articulate them. Obvious examples of such ground rules include procedures for writing up scientific experiments, or conventions of poetic form. However, the issue is much broader than this.

At their broadest, ground rules refer to all the assumptions and expectations we have in relation to an activity. One example considered by Barnes and Sheeran concerns a social studies lesson in which the teacher explained that there are two kinds of family: nuclear and extended. How might students respond to this? If one's parent is a university professor of sociology, perhaps with a degree of enthusiasm. After all, this sounds like proper sociology, a valued activity that brings with it long holidays, international travel and even a limited degree of fame. In any case, 'this is easy...'. On the other hand, many students are likely to react in bemusement. They live in streets containing many kinds of family, none of

---

[34] For example, see Wittgenstein's *Remarks on the Foundations of Mathematics* (Oxford: Blackwell, 1956) and its application to the teaching context by Yvette Solomon (1998) in Teaching Mathematics: ritual, principle and practice, *Journal of Philosophy of Education* 32/3, 377–391. Also, more generally, Lave, J. and Wenger, E. (1991) *Situated Learning: legitimate peripheral participation*, Cambridge: Cambridge University Press.

[35] Barnes, D. and Sheeran, Y. (1991) *School Writing*, Buckingham: Open University Press.

[36] Feldman, C.F., in Bruner and Haste (eds) (1987) Chapter 7: The Linguistic Construction of Cognitive Representations, pp. 131–146 (see Note 2).

which they have ever heard of referred to by these terms. Anyway, is not 'nuclear' something to do with bombs?

Barnes and Sheeran's argument is simple and compelling. As experts, teachers fail to teach the things they take for granted, and thus 'preach to the converted'. For teachers fully to succeed in promoting thinking requires sensitivity to both the forms in which thought is enunciated (subjects, topics, rhetorics), and the assumptions students have, or are likely to have, about what is introduced. It is the rules of a language game that have to be learnt, rather than the details of any particular playing of it.

Learning to Choose

Risk assessment is central to living, and success requires being prepared to take calculated risks. There is, after all, always a risk attached to not taking a risk.

In a world of increasing individualization of risk, the educator's role in developing skills of risk taking becomes crucial. However, risk involves choice. Over-prescription in education can result in passivity and indifference, and in students merely finding all their excitement outside the educational context, so that schools and colleges cease to be rich learning environments.

In broad terms, one might define the areas of potential choice for students of all ages as follows:

(i)   Choice within curriculum areas: choices about how to do certain pieces of work and what pieces of work to do;
(ii)   Choice between curriculum areas: subject and course choice;
(iii) Choice beyond the formal curriculum: in social, sporting and other extra-curricular areas, and in relation to (what might otherwise be) the 'hidden curriculum' of everyday school and college norms.

Given the central roles of choice and risk in (post)modern societies, it can be argued that it is the duty of educators to plan for the development of choosing and risk-taking strategies in each of these three areas. The following criteria might be employed.[37]

Firstly, educational provision can take account of legal assumptions. The operation of the legal system within any country is effectively geared towards certain assumptions concerning the readiness of young people to take responsibility. In England and Wales, for example, the ages of 14, 16,

---

[37] Adapted from Stables, A. (1996) *Subjects of Choice: the process and management of pupil and student choice*, London: Cassell, pp. 228–229.

17 and 18, each signal new points of responsibility. Broadly speaking, children need to take responsibility for their own actions under the law by 14 (at the latest), are free to marry at 16, can drive at 17 and have the vote at 18. Educational policy and practice should help to prepare young people for such responsibilities.

Secondly, there is the issue of international competitiveness. Education systems have undergone significant shifts around the world in order for each country to feel it is 'competing on a level playing field' with its trading partners. Globalization brings increasing expectations regarding international ism in educational provision. Its effects have already become apparent in several areas: in 'credential inflation' at 16 and 18+, as countries such as Britain attempt to match others in the proportion of the population graduating from high school with university entrance qualifications; in widening access to higher education for those with less traditional backgrounds; and in the increased status given to the vocational curriculum. Alongside competitiveness is co-operation: young people are growing up as global citizens with social responsibilities beyond the boundaries of their own nations, so need to understand practices elsewhere, if not emulate them. While this book argues for diversity, this does not imply ignorance of other, related practices.

Thirdly, while there are many constraints on the potential offering of student choice, perhaps the greatest is that of the maturity level of the students themselves. However, whether they are intellectually and morally ready for increasingly responsible choices must be partly dependent on their previous educational experiences, unless we adhere to deficit views of childhood generally. It is therefore important that, throughout school, an emphasis is put on developing a capacity for responsible choice in young people. This is always an imperfect art: full maturity in decision making can never be reached. (How many adults are perfect decision-makers?) Perhaps most obviously, this implies a gradual preparation for the really big choices that become inevitable in the senior years. To take a significant example, choice between subjects and courses can be prepared for through choices within subjects and courses: choices stepped in significance but always carrying real consequences for the chooser.

Education for choice (at least, for conscious choice) implies richness of educational dialogue; rich educational dialogue needs a capacity for criticality. Education is, above all, discursive practice. It is to this realization that we now attend.

Chapter 4

Words, Words, Words: the decentred subject of education

This chapter examines the role of language in constructing and reflecting educational values, both within and beyond the policy sphere, as commonly understood.[1]

According to Wittgenstein, we cannot effectively separate thinking and language.[2] 'Education' is not only a word, but also a whole discourse, the key elements of which, as we interpret them, both define and reflect our educational values.[3] As with childhood, so with educational policy, recent thinking has problematized old assumptions. Jacques Derrida has written of meaning being 'deferred', coining the term 'différance' to combine ideas of difference and deferment.[4] While many have found little positive to say about the group of thinkers commonly known as 'postmodern', but often more accurately described as 'poststructuralist' (Lyotard,[5] Derrida, Levinas[6] and others), their work has served to question the stability and validity of cherished beliefs and values. Derrida means by différance that we can never 'pin down' the meaning of a term, because meaning is always an act of interpretation, and contexts for interpretation are never identical. While many people find Derrida's thinking counter-intuitive regarding apparently

---

1 Permission has been granted by Blackwell Publishers to reproduce material in this chapter from Stables, A. (1998) 'Proximity and Distance: moral education and mass communication', *Journal of Philosophy of Education* 32/3, pp. 399–407.
2 See discussion at end of Chapter 3.
3 See, for example, Norman Fairclough's consideration of the embedding of the idea of 'enterprise' into educational discourse in the 1980s in (1995) *Critical Discourse Analysis*, London: Longman, pp. 112–129.
4 Derrida, J. (1978) *Writing and Difference*, London: Routledge and Kegan Paul.
5 Lyotard, J-F. (1984) *The Postmodern Condition: a report on knowledge*, Manchester: Manchester University Press; also (1988) *Le Différend: phrases in dispute*, Minneapolis: Minnesota: University of Minnesota Press.
6 For an introduction to Levinas's surprisingly (to some) ethical poststructuralism, see Davis, C. (1996) *Levinas: an introduction*, Cambridge: Polity. To Levinas, the self is inscribed as an ethical subject only in relation to the unknowability of the Other.

unarguable concepts such as 'tree' or 'fish', few would argue that terms such as 'beauty', 'truth' and, I would argue, 'education', are qualitative and extremely difficult to define with any degree of accuracy. Where it is possible to create a degree of consensus about such terms, through agreement about the status of numerous concrete examples or manifestations, the term itself relates to nothing that can be seen, heard, touched, smelt, tasted or measured. Education exists in discursive, rather than physical, space. We can cite a beautiful sunset as an example of beauty, but this does not mean that we can determine what every sunset should look like by extrapolating from an idea of beauty; nor can we prescribe what every school should be from our ideas of education. Indeed, as philosophers down the ages have argued, our experiences of the beautiful and the sublime depend on encounter with the unexpected and the transcendental.[7]

What constitutes good education, therefore, really is a matter of opinion. (This is not, of course, to argue that everybody's opinion is granted equal importance regarding matters of this sort.) As regards intangibles such as 'education' and its relation to 'goodness', meaning is developed through, and dependent on values, and is undeniably neither purely objective nor solely subjective. As with 'beauty' and 'kindness', the meanings of such terms, while they may well be rooted in direct sensory experience, are clearly open to cultural and personal interpretation. Similarly, in the case of education, good practice cannot be entirely predetermined by previous examples. While many argue that good examination results make a good school, for example, many others argue that this is a false measure, yet their searches for 'value-added' measures are equally prone to counter-argument.[8] A 'good education' is ultimately something that must be experienced, and the best schools will always exceed any particular expectations we have of them. What is more, the evaluation of educational experience will always be subject to cultural and personal variation.

---

[7] An eighteenth century distinction, manifest to some degree in both Kant's *Critique of Judgment* and Burke's *A Philosophical Enquiry into the Origin of our Ideas of the Sublime and the Beautiful*, distinguishes between these two terms along these lines: the beautiful corresponds to our ideas about order and harmony, and promotes feelings of enjoyment and safety; the sublime, in its magnificence, exceeds our capacity to understand or control it, and thus both amazes and threatens. Thus a volcano may be sublime; a primrose beautiful. Both beauty and sublimity surprise us.

[8] As a complex and, furthermore, as an imagined system, the workings of a school cannot simply be explained in terms of the interaction of pre-specified variables. While research will inevitably identify common patterns between complex systems, this does not imply that variables can be abstracted and applied in terms of predictive explanatory power, however sophisticated the statistical model. See, for example, Byrne, D. (2001) 'Beyond Multilevel Modelling', paper delivered at *British Educational Research Association*, Leeds, September.

Much recent talk of 'evidence-based practice' and an 'applied science of teaching' serves to give both teaching and the study of education a spurious scientific status. It can be argued that this is 'scientistic', rather than 'scientific' thinking: it merely 'sounds like science'. In the broadest sense, of course, educational studies can be seen as social science, but value-laden, interpretive activities such as teaching and educational research cannot operate according to the strictures of 'hard' mathematical positivism, as practised traditionally in fields such as biology and chemistry, however sophisticated the statistical techniques involved. Numbers can only measure the numerically measurable; marking sunsets out of ten is always a tricky business, and beauty even trickier. Rather than an applied science, it would be more valid to speak of an applied politics of education, and politics is not natural science, though political studies do, like educational studies, employ quantitative methods. However, these quantitative methods (surveys, for example) are used to make qualitative judgments.

According to Jean-Francois Lyotard's *The Postmodern Condition*, we have lost faith in the 'grand narratives' (*'grands récits'*) of modernity. Among these is an unquestioned belief in scientific discovery as progress, applicable to the common good. Our assumptions about the unquestioned good of education and schooling are surely part and parcel of this belief in science and progress. In a period when science is seen as exploitative of both people and non-human nature in ways that are bad as well as good, it is not surprising that there is scepticism about the purposes and practices of education. Again, it is not necessary to sympathise with Lyotard's extreme generalization to appreciate some validity in this position. Belief in education as an engine of progress may also be challenged by the increasing difficulties faced by young people in outperforming their parents, compared with much of the twentieth century, at least in the affluent West. It is not now so easy to ensure that education yields a return on your cultural capital.[9]

---

[9] To use Pierre Bourdieu's work in a way of which he would very likely have disapproved, it could be argued that effective schooling for many people will be assessed in terms of return on cultural capital, along the lines of 'My schooling was very good for me; I was the first member of my family to get into university'. (Bourdieu, P. (1997) Forms of Capital, in Halsey, A.H., Lauder, H., Brown, P. and Stuart Wells, A. (eds) *Education: Culture, Economy, Society* Oxford: Oxford University Press, 46–58; Stables, A. (2002) Diachronic and Synchronic Analysis of Education: taking account of the life-history, *Westminster Studies in Education* 25/1, 59–66.) A former Labour Party leader in Britain, Neil Kinnock, indeed used this example to justify state schooling in a pre-election speech in 1992, presumably without considering the counter-argument that if schooling is to be assessed according to greater success than one's forebears, existing levels of social inequality are likely to be maintained or even increased with respect to each succeeding peer group.

Given the intangibility of educational value, we should not be surprised that the language of educational policy is as 'political' (i.e. manipulative and/or ill-defined) as any other political language. The critical discourse analyst, Norman Fairclough, has described successful political slogans as having high 'ambivalence potential': in other words, by their very vagueness they become attractive to a wide range of people who then choose to 'buy into' them.[10]

In the educational debate, several such terms have had their potential for ambiguity further increased by their use in compounds, often with terms that imply inherent contradiction. Thus the Conservative British Prime Minister of the early 1990s, John Major, argued for 'parity of esteem' between vocational and academic courses for 14 to 19–year-olds, knowing full well, perhaps, that, while 'parity' implies a flat equality, 'esteem' demands judgments of relative merit. More recently, there has been much concern with 'sustainable development', a compound term suggesting both fixity ('sustainable') and change ('development').

There are several senses in which educational policies can be seen as paradoxical. The element of paradox can be introduced intentionally or unintentionally. As was pointed out in a critique of educational policy in Canada some years ago, the policy group devising a slogan always 'has its own interests to be served', and this often involves appealing to as broad a band of potential support as possible – sometimes to people with contrary aspirations and ideals.[11] John Codd has made a similar point about New Zealand, arguing that 'conflicting ethical frameworks' of social democrats and neo-liberals caused problems with curriculum reform.[12] To David Corson, the problem is not so much conscious manipulation by policy-makers as 'secondary elaborations of belief by those implementing the policies'.[13] This is a way of acknowledging that context determines meaning, and that the same espoused policy will inevitably be interpreted differently as contexts change.

I have elaborated elsewhere on the problems associated with evaluating equality of opportunity with respect to subject and course choices.[14] Here, one of the most rhetorically charged policy directives of the twentieth century

---

[10] Fairclough, N. (1995) *Critical Discourse Analysis*, London: Longman, pp. 112–129.
[11] Walter, W. (1991) 'Defining Curriculum Policy Through Slogans', *Journal of Education Policy* 6/2, 225–238.
[12] Codd, J. (1993) 'Equity and Choice: the paradox of New Zealand educational reform', *Curriculum Studies* 1/1, 75–90.
[13] Corson, D. (1988) 'Making the Language of Education Policies More User-Friendly', *Journal of Education Policy* 3/3, 249–260.
[14] Stables, A. (1996) *Subjects of Choice: the process and management of pupil and student choice*, London: Cassell; and (1996) 'Paradox in Compound Educational Policy Slogans', *British Journal of Educational Studies* 44/2, 159–167.

can be interpreted in quite contrary ways with respect to measurable outcomes. At its simplest, the problem in this case can be summarized with respect to the following example: if more men than women wish to become engineers, is this a) evidence that equality of opportunity has not been achieved, since the numbers are significantly out of balance, or b) evidence that equality of opportunity has been achieved, since both genders are equally free to choose whether or not to study engineering? Numerical evidence cannot solve such a qualitative dilemma, though, of course, increasingly sophisticated statistical techniques can yield more and more information for us to interpret: for instance, how successful do female engineers tend to be in terms of professional advancement? No such data can do more than influence what must always remain essentially a subjective, or (at most) intersubjective answer to the central question, however.

Educational practice is shot through with assumptions about the fixity of terms that are not fixed. For example, let us consider distance (used in education in the technical sense of 'distance education' and also in the everyday vernacular of life inside and outside the classroom). Because of mass communications, what was far away is now near to hand. This may seem a trivial point, until we consider how our value-systems are laden with ideas relating to proximity and distance: we 'keep our distance' or 'get close to' people; we are 'nearly there' or 'have a long way to go'. Changes in access and notions of proximity and distance problematize, among other things, our ideas about moral development. More broadly, the language we use relates to our real experience of time, place and action. In this case, what constitutes proximity and distance determines, in some sense, how we see our roles as global citizens.

We can find in English literature examples of how the changes of the last hundred years in the above areas can be seen as related to the nature of the moral issues confronting individuals and the language in which they are couched. Laurie Lee marks the end of a long era in *Cider with Rosie*, in which 'Our horizon of woods was the limit of our world'.[15] He notes the change in his Gloucestershire village as really apparent from the late-1920s: 'the end of a thousand years' life', in which the horse's 'eight miles an hour was the limit of our movements'; an end marked by the intrusion of motorised transport into rural life, a movement that was to result in the village becoming 'no more than a place for pensioners' by the middle of the Century,[16] though since the writing of *Cider With Rosie,* it has no doubt become a place for commuters too.

---

[15] Lee, L. (1962) *Cider With Rosie*, London: Penguin, p. 42.
[16] *Ibid.* ps. 216, 217.

In some important respects, the world evoked by Lee is the world of many of the novels of the eighteenth and nineteenth centuries. It is a world in which:

(i)   a few key individuals interact with each other and meet very few other people;
(ii)   a small number of physical settings is involved;
(iii)   the bonds between individuals (whether sentimental or otherwise) are assumed to be long-lasting and to carry expectations of mutual duty;
(iv)   communities are small and status within them is taken largely as a given;
(v)   wealth is passed on through the family, so that the use of material resources is seen as an issue of personal responsibility, and thus an intrinsically moral issue in a sense not applicable to a society in which much wealth is automatically passed on to strangers through imposed taxation;
(vi)   key opportunities and life-chances are rare but to some extent predictable, can often be anticipated some time in advance, and the choices relating to them are made after a good deal of personal reflection and advice;
(vii)   there is a largely unquestioned moral ideal, involving strong Christian belief, self-control and a sense of duty, which for many finds expression in a strong Protestant work ethic.

Typically, in the pre-twentieth century novel, we see a main character's life as a continuous whole, in few geographical locations, punctuated by a small number of critical incidents involving a small number of other characters (with whom, on the whole, the main character enjoys fairly long-lasting relationships), decisions in relation to which are taken (if taken wisely) after a good deal of soul-searching. Occasionally, as in the epistolary novel (such as Richardson's *Pamela*[17]), characters develop relationships other than through direct and sustained physical contact with those living near them, but this is very much the exception rather than the rule; generally only the letter allows for such contact. In such novels, where travel occurs, it is slow and full of incident, and each journey is a highly significant event: note both the significance and the slowness of the journeys (by foot) of Thomas Hardy's protagonists in *Tess of the Durbervilles* and *Jude the Obscure*, to take examples from the late 19th century.[18] The case might be made for an exception in the picaresque novel, which originated in 16th century Spain but is more closely associated with the 18th century in

---

[17] Richardson, S. (1926) *Pamela* Vols. I, II, London: Dent.
[18] Editions by Macmillan (Basingstoke), both 1974.

England. Here locations are more numerous, more effortlessly reached, and more frivolously eschewed. However, this easy journeying is part of the lot of the 'ingenious rogues...who eventually repent the errors of their ways';[19] it is the stuff of comedy and satire. (In Fielding's case, the satire extends to making his 'rogue', Tom Jones, more virtuous than those who taunt him. This playing with the genre may well have been informed by the debates surrounding the potential educational value of travel following the publication of Locke's *Essay Concerning Human Understanding* in 1690.[20]) Trouble waits in store for such gadabouts, however, and they will eventually settle down. Doubtless, part of the charm of hero-villains such as Tom Jones may well be that they have the joie-de-vivre which results in (for the time) fast and frequent travel, and there is a sense in which the picaresque novel may thus prefigure the rootlessness of later modernity, as well as the pre-Enlightenment worldview that, in general, was sceptical of the educational value of travelling. Nevertheless, in *Tom Jones*, relationships are elaborately developed as a small group of characters continually re-engage with each other in a variety of places; the settings do indeed change, but often merely to allow the same protagonists to regroup under modified circumstances.

The continued popularity of the novels of Fielding, Hardy, Dickens, Austen and others is borne out by the recent spate of television and feature films of their work. Nevertheless, the preoccupation of each of these writers is with moral issues arising in a context in some respects radically different from that of a child growing up at the turn of the Millennium. Specifically, the modern child encounters many individuals physically from beyond the local community and the family circle, including those with alternative social mores, religions, speech habits, dress etc., and is exposed to people and events indirectly, via the mass media, from many parts of the world.

Both the physically real and virtual, or vicarious, lives of children have been revolutionised by mass communication. Possibilities for travel and new cultural and interpersonal experiences are increased. In terms of vicarious experience, the current situation puts new forms of moral pressure on the child. First, there is pressure to care about events thousands of miles distant, in contexts of which the child has no direct physical experience, and where assumptions and moral norms are different. News broadcasts, including those made specifically for children, place a burden of responsibility on the young to prevent starvation, disease and conflict wherever the mass media have

---

19 Drabble, M. and Stringer, J. (eds) (1987) *The Concise Oxford Companion to English Literature*, Oxford: Oxford University Press, quotation from p. 439.

20 Fielding, J. (1985) *The History of Tom Jones*, Harmondsworth: Penguin. Locke argued that experience and association (and therefore travel) produced learning, an idea that was to influence the Romantic movement and much modern thinking about education. (See Chapter 3.)

access to it. Second, children are given easy access to scenes of violence, suffering and depravity to which they were not formerly exposed unless they were encountered domestically. In this virtual world of easy access and uncertain responsibility, some fear the danger of a 'cyborg' mentality, 'guided and programmed by a military-industrial logic that need[s] no translation into the Hobbesian language of competitive human relations', to quote Andrew Ross's response to the film *Terminator*:[21] a mentality which simply avoids moral complexity through dehumanisation. In addition, children are encouraged into a sense of environmental and ecological responsibility that relates immediate and local concerns to global and conceptual issues: the conservation of species, global warming, the use of sustainable resources and the like. Each of these facets of contemporary life is a potential source of both ethical and psychological conflict for the child.

Moral educators have tended to pay little direct attention to proximity and distance as analogues of moral choice, though environmentalists have noted the relationship of issues of physical scale to moral concerns.[22]

To state that moral choices are 'affected' by scale and proximity is not necessarily to claim that all moral choices can be *conceived of* in terms of scale and proximity, even though our vernacular is riddled with phrases such as 'getting under the skin of', 'being close to' and 'keeping your distance' which imply, if not specifically moral concerns, at least that the expression of individual values consists in part of choices concerning how 'close' we want to get to each other or how 'closely' we want to be involved in projects, debates etc.

While little may have been written on this specifically in the field of moral education, there has been a broader philosophical and epistemological interest in boundaries and limits in relation to cultural norms and values. At its bleakest, poststructuralism has encouraged a worldview in which all old polarities, such as distance and proximity, can be deconstructed to the extent that we almost cannot know 'where we stand'. Baudrillard, for example, presents a society in which consumerism has replaced production to the extent that we live in an aimless world of signs, competing only to seduce us: a sort of terrifying proximity of pointless temptation.[23] In a world in

---

[21] Ross, A. (1994) *The Chicago Gangster Theory of Life*, London: Verso, p. 233.

[22] Thus, in her commentary on the work of David Orr and others, Madhu Suri Prakesh notes that 'Nel Noddings cautions us that our ability to care for others is profoundly affected by the elements of scale and proximity'. Prakash, M.S. (1995) Ecological Literacy for Moral Virtue: Orr on (moral) education for postmodern sustainability, *Journal of Moral Education* 24/1, 3–18, quotation from p.15; Orr, D. (1992) *Ecological Literacy: education and the transition to a postmodern world*, Albany: SUNY Press.

[23] Gane, M. (1991) *Baudrillard: critical and fatal theory*, London: Routledge.

which children can no longer name the trees and flowers in their own gardens, but have in-depth knowledge of a *Star Wars*-style mythological outer universe, traditional assumptions about proximity and distance do indeed seem to have broken down. This disorientation is of little help to any who wish to cling to the belief of the possibility of any moral education. A potentially helpful discussion here is provided by Derrida in *Aporias* (1993), where he examines the 'limits of Truth', in particular the limits of one's ownership of one's own life. Here, Derrida affirms, in typical Derridean fashion, that identity depends upon difference, that reality must exceed its limits (of which there are three kinds: cultural, political and linguistic; of 'domains of discourse'; and of concepts and terms); and that, ultimately, death is the possibility of the impossible.[24]

Of course, language is very important here. Much of Derrida's argument typically relies upon a serious playing with words, and an exploration of paradox. He states that understanding of the self is always related to an appreciation of the otherness of the other: 'it is always by *starting from* the idiomatic hereness of my language, my culture and my belongings that I relate myself to the difference of the over there.'[25]

This, of course, raises moral issues. If language is an expression or aspect of culture, or even is culture itself, then debates about meaning are debates about cultural norms and values both reflect and help to create moral codes; however, different codes can never completely coincide. Derrida's own concern is not directly with the moral implications of these issues, other than stating that, as we approach death, 'dasein' (Heidegger's term for existential being) should be 'expecting and waiting for death...and waiting for itself there', given that death is 'no-longer-being-able-to-be-there'.[26] Perhaps to live well, we should acknowledge the possibility of the impossible, and acknowledge our anxiety concerning it. This in turn implies that although there are no single scientific answers to the questions we are engaged with, we can at least employ our reasoning and alter the realities of our existence as a result. This is, at any rate, the germ of a more optimistic view than Baudrillard's.

In many senses, the modern, or postmodern, child not only has to come to terms with the possibility of the impossibility of death (in fact, in this respect, children in former ages must have been more than equally challenged), but is in a position to access, or even bring about, the impossible, in the sense of gaining access physically to many foreign

---

[24] Derrida, J. (1993) *Aporias*, Stanford, California: Stanford University Press, ps. 1, 6, 10, 23, 73ff.

[25] *Ibid.* p. 52.

[26] *Ibid.* ps. 69, 68.

cultures and both physically and virtually to much that is potentially emotionally and psychologically disturbing.

The issue of where we place our boundaries, or find them placed, and which ones we cross, lies at the heart of all moral debate. In a world of hugely increased potential access via mass communication, 'how do we teach children to be good?'.[27] At this point, it may be helpful to consider Straughan's tripartite model for teachers (that they must teach *that*, *how* and *to*...), and discuss this in terms of issues of proximity and distance.

'Teaching that' in the contemporary context must surely involve developing a critical awareness of the mass media, by informing children of its structures, functions and processes, both technically and sociopolitically. Children might also learn about the history of mass transport and mass communications, and how these have altered patterns of life over recent decades (and are continuing so to do). The 'teaching that' element in this case has obvious implications for the teaching of geography, history and 'communication' in the junior years, and can be dealt with in almost every curriculum area later on, including both arts and sciences.

By 'teaching how...', Straughan is referring to the capability to 'Make up one's own mind in the light of relevant information', and he notes that this is not a capacity which is easy to impart directly, especially to young children. Straughan suggests 'value neutrality' and 'values clarification' as key teaching strategies in general here, although young children may only be able to deal with this within a limited range of conceptual frameworks (for example, with reference to what is 'fair' or 'unfair', or in response to the question, 'What would it be like if *everyone* behaved like that?').[28] Straughan also stresses the need to give young children plenty of the sort of factual information, which can inform specific moral choices.

Essentially, this form of teaching is concerned with empowering students to make decisions within a moral framework. Many such decisions, in the contemporary context, can be framed in terms of issues of proximity and distance. We might summarise these as issues of travel and of access, though the two ideas clearly overlap.

The following questions (which imply a good deal of 'teaching that' as well as 'teaching how') exemplify the former category. When, and under what circumstances, do the advantages of using the motor car outweigh the disadvantages (both social and ecological)? What should be done to ease traffic congestion, and to reduce air pollution?

These are questions that can be posed to students of all ages, with varying degrees of contextualizing information and at varying levels of

---

[27] Roger Straughan (1982) *Can We Teach Children to be Good? Basic issues in moral, personal and social education*, Milton Keynes: Open University Press.
[28] *Ibid*. ps. 106, 108.

sophistication, without prescribing the most desirable outcomes of the deliberation. The young child can become aware that chemicals in exhaust fumes can be bad for your health (and for buildings), for example, but this still allows for multiple perspectives on the problem, and a myriad of possible solutions; the more advanced student might consider the social, economic and ecological advantages of using alternative fuels, or issues relating to potential forms of government intervention in the use of private transport, again issues the exploration of which encourages the realisation and balancing of a plurality of perspectives.

Issues of access imply questions such as the following. Should certain things be kept private? When should you try to find things out, or gain physical access to them, and when should you respect others' privacy? Such issues are pivotal to any ethical exploration of proximity and distance, and require for their consideration heightened sensitivities towards both self and other.

Mass transport and mass communication have hugely increased people's capacity to access information, from encyclopedias to child pornography. Very young children might begin by considering what things should be private. When is it unfair to 'tell on' someone? When should we keep a secret? What kind of people should young children reply to when they talk to them and what should they say in return? What is the difference between taking and stealing?

Clearly, the issues for older students are many and complex here, and are rendered increasingly important in a culture which, despite its increasing individualization, does not always allow for reasoned reflection before action, such is the speed at which it conducts its communications. (Proximity and distance across time as well as space have been problematized.) The loosening and diversification of sexual and other *mores* means that moral education must be as much a critical reflection as a preparation. Certainly, few children will defer using the internet until they have discussed its potential uses and abuses. Interesting starting points for the teacher might concern the relative rights of press freedom and individual privacy, censorship, and what moral obligations, if any, we have in our use of the internet, and in our capacity to access new databases, whether to target individuals for promotional mail-shots, or to tamper with their bank accounts. Issues of access also include such concerns as rights to walk in the countryside and rights to access goods from other parts of the world, both of which can feasibly be addressed in the secondary curriculum and have strong moral elements.

As far as 'teaching to..' is concerned, Straughan stresses that the main factor determining whether people *act as* moral agents is motivation, and this in turn implies that they must see 'moral behaviour....in as desirable a light as possible' and that they must have a genuine feeling for others. In the latter case, the key is 'a variety of social experience';[29] in the former, teachers can achieve a great deal through their own examples, by clearly conveying the satisfaction to be gained from doing things well, in the broadest sense of the word (including their own subject teaching). It is important that children learn to base their moral behaviour in an informed empathy, and that they feel there is a point to behaving morally.

Potentially, mass communication presents us with a greatly increased range of social experiences; however, these can be both presented and dealt with in a depersonalised and amoral way. Thus we see harrowing pictures of the victims of war on the television news, but these pictures are soon replaced by others which present no such emotional challenges (or other emotional challenges) and we have been left with no sense of responsibility for what we have witnessed. At the same time, computer games and the like present human aggression in a yet more depersonalized and trivialized context, arguably developing a tradition formerly limited to the cartoon.

Teachers surely have a crucial role here, both in focusing attention on such scenes in a more protracted and reflective manner, and by exploring, but also presenting, possible models of right action in response to them. Teachers are also in the position to help students to deal with a problem that did not greatly concern previous generations: how, or whether, to apportion their compassion with respect to physical distance. While the mass media give us apparently intimate contact with distressing scenes from around the world, should we take the view that 'charity begins at home' and that the further away the problem, the less it is a problem, or should we feel equally responsible for the plight of children in far-away continents as for the deprived of our own towns and cities? Clearly there are no simple answers to such questions, and young people must find their own solutions in their own terms. For schools and colleges not to address such issues, however, would surely imply a blinding naivety concerning current social conditions, as well as being a lost educational opportunity.

As with ideas of proximity and distance, so every assumption relating to education changes from time to time, place to place, culture to culture, even person to person. At the same time, there can be no 'private language', as Wittgenstein forcefully argued in the *Philosophical Investigations*. Our conceptions of education must be culturally determined, but this is not to say that they can be fixed or immutable. An attention to the language of education, and to language as interpretation, therefore, leads the policy debate far away from some of the easy assumptions that have driven it, in the UK and elsewhere, in recent years. ('Proximity' and 'distance', indeed, have scarcely featured as policy language.) Education is, or should be,

---

[29] *Ibid.* ps. 112, 116.

bigger than all our attempts to account for it, as the shifting meanings of words relating to qualitative aspects of our human experience remind us. Neither education as a subject, nor those subjected to it, should have every aspect of their identities nailed to the cross of accountability, of efficiency, or even of social progress.

In the context of globalization, an important area of shifting emphasis and interpretation concerns the role of education in nation-building, and it is to this issue, of central and acknowledged importance to policy makers, that the next chapter is devoted.

Chapter 5

Schooling, the Nation and 'The Culture'

School systems are generally conceived of in national terms, even though there may be intercultural variation within nations regarding educational expectations and norms; to a lesser extent, this is also true of higher education. This chapter argues for devolved educational decision-making, with actors at each level of policy formulation and implementation encouraged to interpret current trends in their institutional contexts. This implies an acceptance that tensions such as that between community and competition must always be transacted yet can never be resolved.

Educational policy and practice have always been organized privately, locally or nationally, with reference to policies and practices in other, often competing, nations. Only with the development of a bureaucratic framework for international schools, organized loosely around the International Baccalaureate programme, has the formal organization of education happened to any degree at international level; this notwithstanding, most international schools remain largely autonomous, private institutions catering for the children of international élites, the direct impact of which on the lives of local populations is difficult to ascertain. There has been debate recently about the degree to which internationalism in education (as, indeed, in other spheres) is, in any case, a viable or valid concept. After all, globalization can be read as promoting certain national, rather than international, cultures on the world stage; by the same token, international schools are seen by some as little more than 'American (or whatever) schools abroad'.[1]

What is unarguable is that cultures are often understood nationally. This remains so even in a globalized world: we still talk of French cooking, Japanese art and Brazilian Carnival, and of national cultural influences. Educational practice, as a form of cultural practice, is bound to reflect cultural differences that are often conceived of in national terms. This is not to imply, of course, that any of the key terms in this debate – culture, nation, education – have stable parameters.

---

[1] For an overview of current debates around international education and international schools, see Hayden, M. and Thompson, J.J. (2000) (eds) *International Schools and International Education: improving teaching, management and quality*, London: Kogan Page.

National cultures, as well as being unstable, are often not quite synonymous with nation states, however, and the latter generally play key roles in educational policy and planning, with greater or lesser devolvement to regions and other interest groups (such as religious bodies). Education tends to be formally organized, particularly at the macro level, with respect to political, rather than cultural, forms of national organization. When, in the 1970s, Denis Lawton stressed the need for the curriculum to transmit a common culture (a rallying cry of many conservative thinkers about education since), he, similarly, overlooked this distinction.[2]

Education also tends to be organized, and made accountable, with reference to certain regulative ideals, including economic needs, 'standards', equality of opportunity and social justice, with governments of Left and Right tending to pay differential attention to various combinations of these. However, globalization poses significant problems for education thus conceived on two fronts.

Firstly, the very existence of felt needs to ensure any form of equality, or imposed definition of standard, is a partial admission that educational policy operates cross-culturally, since the debate is as much concerned with equal treatment of groups as of individuals, and there is no taken-for-granted consensus about educational value. In a truly homogenous culture, such ideals would be unnecessary. Furthermore, the more diversified a nation state becomes, the more attention may be paid to the need to ensure cultural coherence through education, as is apparent in the emphasis on 'cultural literacy' in the United States in the 1980s and on the debate about national heritage in the National Curriculum in England and Wales in the 1990s.[3] This is not, however, the inevitable response to globalization and multi-culturalism: alternative strategies include various forms of decentralization and/or emphasis on process skills, such as critical analysis, rather than prescribed content, in the curriculum.

---

[2] Lawton, D. (1973) *Social Change, Educational Theory and Curriculum Planning*, Milton Keynes: Open University Unibooks.

[3] The earlier association of 'cultural literacy' with promoters of minority cultures such as Paolo Freire and C.A. Bowers (though the two are opposed in many ways) was challenged, particularly in the United States, by the publication of E.D. Hirsch's (1987) *Cultural Literacy: what every American needs to know* (Boston: Houghton Mifflin), resulting in a dominant view of cultural literacy as the ability to share meanings held as standard among the dominant culture of a nation state. This perspective was influential in the debates of the 1980s and 1990s in Britain about the role of the National Curriculum in the transmission and preservation of national heritage, a role that has gone largely unchallenged in many countres, where education is strongly seen as a form of nation building (e.g. Marum, 1996; Phillips, 1998 – see Chapter 2, Note 13).

Secondly, and perhaps more obviously, people increasingly construct their identities in more-than-national terms. The author of this book is English, British, European and 'Western' – and 'international', in the sense that, like very many people nowadays, I frequently cross national boundaries and have business and personal associates in a number of countries. I cannot, therefore, conceive of notions of success, fairness or justice only with respect to Britain (or England). Our frames of reference are not neatly bounded by nation states.

Social theory has, of course, acknowledged this, and has responded to it in a number of ways, not always by arguing that the powers of the nation state should be reduced. Both Third Way political thinking and traditional European conservatism, for example, have continued to stress the importance of nation states in providing necessary regulation and protection with respect to globalization. Anthony Giddens, guru of the British Third Way, ostensibly practised by New Labour, has argued for the State's role to increase in response to globalization, rather than the reverse.[4]

The argument here, specific to education (though not irrelevant to other spheres) is that the nation state is increasingly untenable as the main agent of educational policy, other than at the lightest level of facilitation, and is ill-advised to pursue the increasing centralization of educational practice, in the form of stipulation of teaching and assessment practices, again other than at the 'light touch' level of attempting to draw baselines in terms of minimal core curriculum provision and standardization of qualifications that share common titles. As complex, culturally driven systems, schools and other educational institutions are generally best understood by those with strong local knowledge, at least as far as questions regarding institutional policies and practices are concerned.[5]

The State clearly has a role, as it does in other spheres, in ensuring that people are not cheated or misled. Beyond this, however, State regulation runs

---

4 See both *The Third Way* (1999) and *The Third Way and its Critics* (2000) (both Cambridge: Polity). Giddens' response to disappointments in Third Way politics is often to argue for more state intervention.

5 A full exposition of this argument is developed in Stables, A. (unpublished) *School As Imagined Community: locating and studying institutions in discursive space*, University of Bath. The argument is partly resonant with that of Stephen Ball, whose view of school effectiveness is described as 'heretical' by Hugh Lauder, Felicity Wikeley and Ian Jamieson. See Ball, S.J., 'Educational Studies, Policy Entrepreneurship and Social Theory', in Slee, R., Weiner, G. and Tomlinson, S. (eds) (1998) *School Effectiveness for Whom? Challenges to the School Effectiveness and School Improvement Movements* London: Falmer, 70–83; Ball, S.J. (1996) 'Good School/Bad School', paper at *British Educational Research Association*, Lancaster, September; Lauder, H., Wikeley, F. and Jamieson, I., 'Models of Effective Schools: limits and capabilities', in Slee *et al* (1998), pp. 50–69.

an increasing risk of becoming counter-productive, because 'education' is a qualitative concept and its meaning, worth and effectiveness are all matters of interpretation. Implicitly, policy makers acknowledge this by making their rallying cries as all-embracing as possible (see Chapter 4). Explicitly, they often, sometimes aided and abetted by educationalists, further the myths of 'good schools', 'effectiveness' and 'evidence-based practice', often justified as in the pursuit of lofty ideals, yet without bothering to ask, 'for whom?', or only asking it in the most selective of ways. There is a danger that, if equal treatment does not result in equal achievement, we replace the reductionist sociology underpinning interventionist policies with an even more reductionist social determinism. Meanwhile, in countries in which they remain free enough so to do, people continue to choose, evaluate and generally take from schools and other education services in accordance with their own tastes and preferences, oblivious to politicians' attempts to force them to think otherwise. This is so because education is a taken, not a given: educational services are offered, but they are differentially received. Education might be seen as a public good, but cannot be regarded uniformly as such.

To stress the role of interpretation in education seems quite in tune with both constructivist and social-constructivist accounts of learning and with contemporary cultural theory. In the spirit of the origins of hermeneutics as the interpretation of literary and religious text, I shall now consider some specific consequences for curriculum, management and policy of an emphasis on both student and teacher as 'reader'.

In terms of curriculum, an emphasis on the reader implies an emphasis on both pupils and teachers as transactors, rather than receivers, of curriculum. To see the learner as reader is also to see the subject as text, however. This is not merely an argument for the recycling of child-centredness, therefore, but an acknowledgment of the importance of the 'sedimented structures' of teaching and learning: of genres, ground rules and language games. Throughout the whole process, both students and teachers are encountering, negotiating and reworking traditions and constraints: ways of thinking, behaving and doing. Good teaching is both deeply traditional and deeply subversive; good learning is grounded in solid knowledge but results in new ways of dealing with the world.

Take first language and literature teaching, for example: the subject known as 'English' in the United Kingdom, though not universally. I have argued elsewhere that approaches to English, particularly in the UK, have been characterized by an unhelpful polarization between Prescriptive and Expressive models, the former stressing correctness in language use and the greatness of the literary canon, the latter the innate creativity of the child.[6]

---

[6] Stables, A. (1992) *An Approach to English*, London: Cassell, pp. 5–11; (1998). Is it Appropriate? *Literacy and Learning*, 2/1, 38–43.

Although English teachers have, for some years now, been urged to adopt a more Descriptive approach, in which 'knowledge about language' (KAL) becomes integral to both language and literature studies, many have found this difficult, tending to annex 'grammar teaching' (and sometimes returning to Prescriptive models) while returning to Expressive approaches, minus KAL, wherever possible. The result can be that large-scale innovations, such as the Literacy Hour for primary schools, while having some effect, produce changes less radical than intended, since teachers tend to negotiate them with respect to their existing values rather than 'take them on board' fully with regard to reconceptualizing their practice. Thus, for example, the emphasis on genre in language and literature teaching, promoted by Gunther Kress, Frances Christie and others, and providing teachers with ways of dealing with literary form that were not prescriptive (Expressive teachers having mistrusted any attention to form), seemed to have only a slow and limited professional impact for some years, despite its potential for bringing the Prescriptive and Expressive traditions together to some degree.[7] Even English or language arts teachers, who may pride themselves on their open-mindedness and potential for creative subversion, have often fallen prey to an either-or view of their subject based more on teachers' philosophy than learners' reality. As elsewhere in education, ideology has found it all too easy to take over from an emphasis on interpretation.

Managers in education need to be interpreters too. If we want them to be seen as good educators, we should encourage them to model the kinds of intelligent interpretation we expect from our students. Looked at this way, educational policy and management become a matter of the interpretation of social trends with respect to the running of educational institutions and the practices of teaching and learning. Issues of globalization, individualization and ecology need, therefore, to be addressed by all the key actors: by politicians, civil servants, school inspectors, senior and middle managers in schools and colleges, and teachers managing their classes. The question is always, 'What does this mean for our institutions and our students?'. In an educationally rich environment, there can be no monopoly of viewpoints on this most demanding of management questions.

Briefly, for my purpose here is not detailed policy prescription, let us consider the often apparently intractable problem of the degree of independence that should be encouraged for schools.

A fully interpretive view of education demands the freedom to interpret for each player in the system. This implies both that over-regulation is counter-productive, and also that none be so disempowered by the system

---

7 For a concise introduction to genre-based approaches to teaching, see Kress, G. and Knapp, P. (1992) 'Genre in a Social Theory of Language', *English in Education* 26 (2) 4–15.

that their freedom to develop their interpretations, including through experiment, is stifled. Poor teaching is the likely outcome of the inability to attract staff into schools characterized as 'failing' within a competitive system that acknowledges only one kind of 'good school': that which achieves high examination grades, whether measured in terms of raw scores or 'added value'; however, such schools may desperately need teachers with the capacity and courage to innovate and take risks.[8]

There is, by contrast, a role for co-operation and mutual support even within a system designed to promote interpretation. As with the teaching of English and other subjects, this sense of balance has often been lost, with the policy debate polarizing between thorough-going egalitarianism and crude 'winner-takes-all' markets. The result of this extreme vacillation in the UK, at least in England, has been, in some ways, the worst of both worlds: a continuing, perhaps increasing tendency for the best results to be gained by fee-paying schools beyond the financial reach of most of the population, and despair and disillusion in inner-city comprehensive schools repeatedly seen as 'failing'. Egalitarian solutions sit uneasily in capitalist societies where wealth must be created as well as distributed, and in which full equality can only realistically be achieved by everyone having nothing, since individual and collective aspirations always ensure unequal results even from the same 'opportunities'; equally, total deregulation could not ensure universal access to educational provision.

A prerequisite to gaining this sense of balance is an acceptance of paradox. Since the postmodern turn, this has become acknowledged in a number of literatures, including that of management.[9] Life is not about resolving one side of a coin into the other, but requires an acceptance that each side acts as a counterbalance. Educational theorists have been unwilling, often, to credit this view, as it effectively problematizes many of their socially reformist ends. Indeed, the belief that certain tensions cannot be resolved has been defined as a traditional characteristic of conservative

---

[8] Perhaps symptomatic of this, *The Times* of June 8th, 2002 carried a piece by Glen Owen (p.12) reporting England's National Association of Head Teachers effectively laying the blame for indiscipline in secondary schools on 'the haemorrhaging of the middle classes' into the private sector as the result, at least in part, of inadequate funding. This can be read as a stark example of the tendency to judge the whole school system with reference to a particular set of middle class values.

[9] In the educational management literature, Mike Wallace has drawn attention to the constant negotiations that are required between competing demands and value positions: Wallace, M. and Hall, V. (1994) *Inside the SMT: Team Approaches to Secondary School Management*, London: Paul Chapman; Wallace, M. and Huckman, L. (1999) *Senior Management Teams in Primary Schools: the quest for synergy*, London: Routledge.

political thought, against which many professional educators, in the UK at least, have become ideologically entrenched.[10] However, acceptance of irresolvable paradox does not preclude change; if anything, it presupposes it. What it does preclude is easy, once-and-for-all change, irrespective of consequence. There is no 'end of history', unless (as Fukuyama has argued) by 'history' we mean the procession of grand ideologies, each claiming the ultimate solution.[11] Change operates within paradox, and does not resolve it.

Two fundamental paradoxes in the educational policy debate are Centralization/Decentralization and Community/Competition. Each of these is ultimately irresolvable, and educational policy should start with recognition of this. Education is thus a collective social concern that depends on and promotes individual difference (at institutional and personal levels); it also involves people and institutions working both with and against each other to achieve better results, just as the trainee teachers the author has taught over the years support each other in the quest for teaching posts for which they are also competitors.

These two paradoxes are so simple they are almost truisms, yet their truth is very often forgotten. Arguments continue to rage over the relative merits of centralizing and decentralizing systems of schooling, rather than over the devolution and sharing of powers in a given context at a given time. Educational Left and Right continue to fight over the relative merits of competition and collaboration between schools, all the while competing against each other while collectively furthering the debate.

To escape modernist ideologies is, at long last, to be able to escape the futile war between government and governed, and between competition and community. At every level, policy should acknowledge that educational institutions are, always have been, and always will be competitive communities, attempting to do better than each other for the ultimate betterment of the system as a whole. Even if we adopt a position that is postmodern to the point of anti-modernism, and replace 'betterment' with mere 'change', then this endless change is driven by the conflicting demands of both competition and community.

Briefly, then, for the detailed prescription of policy to context would be out of step with the argument as a whole, what might we expect of a school as a competitive community?

---

[10] See, for example, Eatwell, R. and Wright, A. (1999) *Contemporary Political Ideologies*, London: Pinter.

[11] Fukuyama claims that ultimately liberal democracy will triumph over all such ideologies, as has already happened in the United States, so bringing 'the end of history' thus understood. Fukuyama, F. (1992) *The End of History and the Last Man*, London: Hamilton.

Firstly, in terms of its dealings with the outside world, it would co-operate with other institutions as and where appropriate, for the short or long term gain of one or both. This might mean the sharing of specialist teachers, perhaps with local business and industry, as well as with schools and colleges. It might mean balancing various sources of funding. It might mean investing disproportionately in certain areas of particular demand and specialist provision.

Secondly, in terms of its internal structures, there would be commitment not only to differentiation, but also to the pursuit of a common cause of difference. This might mean educating in the processes of choice-making and risk-taking, preparing students for the increasing demands of growing up in a world of global lifestyle choices. It might mean abandoning the widely held belief, for which there is little or no evidence, that a 'broad and balanced' curriculum necessarily produces fuller and more balanced human beings. It might mean making students more accountable for the consequences of their own actions.

All the above are possible interpretations of a commitment to inter-pretation itself. They relate to the meso and micro levels of educational policy: the institution, the teacher and the student. At the macro level, these impetuses towards diversity can be all but strangled by crude ways of holding schools to account. This is made even easier for governments where they hold sole responsibility for the funding of education. They can then evaluate schools according to measures, which are at best reductionist and at worst simply misleading. Whether these are simple measures of examination success or some statistically impressive attempt at assessing 'added value', they can never encapsulate the huge variety of criteria employed by parents, students, teachers, employers and others to decide whether educational institutions are succeeding. If there is anyone, or any group of people, that can be thought of as entitled to judge an institution, it surely comprises the stakeholders in, and users of, that institution. This seems a million miles from government policies in Britain and many other countries at the time of writing.

A further advantage of a pragmatic, interpretive approach is that it allows for much greater articulation between policy and curriculum. The educational debate has suffered from a lack of 'joined-up thinking' at the macro and micro levels, with the former dominated by debates about access, social justice and cost-effectiveness and the latter by a view of pedagogy as technical skill, transferable by 'best practice'. Each underplays the central role of interpretation and usefulness to context that a more pragmatic-liberal educational philosophy espouses.

The view promoted in this chapter has been of individuals and self-defined cultural groups developing their voices in the educational debate as interpreters of the contexts they find themselves in. Such development of a voice does not guarantee that all wishes can be granted, but it does promote greater responsiveness and flexibility within the system. In effect, individuals and groups are encouraged thereby to become active critical readers of their contexts. This view of both educator and educated as reader/ interpreter has significant implications for educational thought and planning at all levels, from supra-national policy, via institutional management and curriculum planning, to classroom practice.

Taking further the analogy of interpreter as reader, the following chapter discusses the 'literacies' debate in curriculum planning as a conceptual framework that transcends both child and nation-centredness. This leads into consideration of the third key issue: the ecological challenge.

Chapter 6

Conditional Literacies and the Case for Educational Pragmatism: the use of literacy in curriculum planning

This chapter argues that it is valid to see all forms of understanding as literacies, broadly understood. This being so, it becomes possible to consider various forms of learning as the development of 'disciplined literacies' at various levels. A focus on literacies transcends narrow notions of both the child and the nation.

There has been much appropriation of the term 'literacy' in education, often without theoretical justification. If, however, a conception of literacy is adopted which draws on a Saussurean understanding of language as sign-system (i.e. literacy as semiotics), then it is indeed justifiable to use the term in collocations relating to essentially non-verbal activity (e.g. 'scientific literacy'). Such an acknowledgment can have important ramifications for curriculum policy. At the same time, there are conflicting philosophical traditions that lead toward, at one extreme, an ideal of the 'literate person' and, at the other, extreme relativism and instrumentalism. A pragmatic approach would acknowledge both judgmental and non-judgmental views of literacy, and, by adopting a broad, semiotic view of literacy, would have potential use as framework for curriculum planning.

A.N.Whitehead is reputed to have held that modern thought is a series of footnotes to Plato; certainly many Platonic assumptions are still broadly upheld in the field of education: for example, the high status of mathematics and the pure sciences, and even the fact that the highest form of graduate qualification is usually called 'doctor of philosophy'. However, we are also the children of relativism and social constructivism.[1] Our condition is

---

[1] For an introduction to Whitehead, Whitehead, A.N., Northrop, F.S.C. and Gross, M.W. (1953) *Alfred North Whitehead: an anthology*, New York: Macmillan; to Plato, Pappas, N. (1995) *Routledge Philosophy Guidebook to Plato and the Republic*, London: Routledge; to social constructivism, Berger, P.L. and Luckmann, T. (1966) *The Social Construction of Reality: a treaty in the sociology of knowledge*, New York: Irvington.

characterized by conflicts between our assumptions of absolute good and our conscious need to tolerate. The dichotomy is apparent in our attitudes to literacy. On the one hand, we appreciate that to be literate is no more than to have the ability to recognise and reproduce the signs of a particular medium (usually writing); on the other, we associate literacy with all that is civilized, and illiteracy with all that is unformed. For many (perhaps most famously the development educator, Paolo Freire), literacy is the way to freedom, illiteracy a condemnation to enduring repression.[2] To be illiterate is to be less than fully human.[3] Historically, conservatives, moderate social reformers and revolutionaries have shared this idealistic conception of literacy. Tony Blair's 'Education, Education, Education' slogan prior to the 1997 British General Election, and the subsequent introduction of his government's Literacy Strategy,[4] sits easily alongside the aspirations of both nostalgic conservatives and critical emancipators in this respect.

This ambivalence concerning literacy has deep historical, philosophical and religious roots, going back at least as far as the Socratic distaste for the Sophists and the consequent reduction of the language arts (rhetoric, grammar, logic) to the (trivial) *trivium* of the Medieval European curriculum, while at the same time, Plato argued for Philosopher-Kings trained in dialectic[5] and Judaeo-Christian theology taught that the Word (*logos*) preceded all Creation. At the turn of the fifteenth century, Julian of Norwich, author of *Revelations of Divine Love* wrote (*sic*) that she 'kowde no lettres', yet she produced one of the great works of Christian literature. What did she mean? Perhaps that she could read and write in English, but not Latin, or that her Latin was vernacular; perhaps that she could not read and write at all (for it is possible that her work was dictated); perhaps merely that she did not regard herself as generally highly educated.[6] Whatever the case, she did not

---

[2] A series of books by and about Freire begins with *Pedagogy of the Oppressed*, London: Penguin, 1972. For an overview, see Mayo, P. (1999) *Gramsci, Freire and Adult Education: possibilities for transformative action*, London: Zed.

[3] A compelling, if chilling, account of modernity's incapacity to regard the Other as fully human can be found in Alain Finkielkraut's *In the Name of Humanity: reflections on the Twentieth Century*, London: Pimlico (2001). One of Finkielkraut's challenging assertions is that humanity is no more truly humane than a century ago: we have merely replaced a culture that attempted to exterminate otherness by one in which everyone effectively operates as a tourist; a culture of bland toleration that amounts to little more than indifference and still falls short of genuine respect.

[4] The Literacy Strategy takes various forms, but its most significant innovation has been the commitment of one hour each day to literacy work (under strong guidelines) for all children aged 5 to 11 since 1997 in primary schools.

[5] Plato (ed. Lee) (1987) *The Republic*, Harmondsworth: Penguin.

[6] Julian of Norwich (trans. Spearing, E.) (1998) *Revelations of Divine Love*, London: Penguin.

conceive of herself as literate. In a religious tradition in which the beginning was the Word, and Christ was the Word made flesh, and a philosophical tradition in which only the wise can perceive ideal forms, the distinctions between literacy, reason, wisdom and divinity are not clear. Literacy tends towards greatness, and the humble must not proclaim it too highly; illiteracy, on the other hand, is shame: one step further from greatness, and fit cause for self-flagellation. The literate who misuse their powers are simply evil; hence Plato's scorn, not only for sophistry, but for poetry.[7]

This chapter argues for educational pragmatism regarding literacy. However, 'pragmatism', like 'relativism', can be used pejoratively. It can excuse the basest motives, or mask a failure to take responsibility (though it should be noted that Plato made the same point about democracy in *The Republic*, yet intelligent people still argue for it[8]). It must be stressed here, therefore, that philosophical pragmatists do not oppose the inevitable existence of regulative ideals, nor deny them normative power but rather accept them as beyond logical analysis: as objects of moral and aesthetic, rather than of philosophical, contemplation. On one level, therefore, the views of Plato and the relativists can be squared. Part, at least, of the human species aspires to perfection, good, truth and understanding, yet in a bewildering variety of ways. However, regulative ideals can have no absolute and uncontested justifications. That we are concerned about proving their absolute validity (rather than accepting it, as did Plato) may be a symptom of an unhealthy faith in positivist science: a mixing of language games, in Wittgensteinian terms. To quote Richard Rorty, 'Granted that 'true' is an absolute term, its conditions of application will always be relative. For there is no such thing as belief being justified *sans phrase...*'.[9] According to Rorty, in so far as human progress is possible, it is made so by the devotion of our powers of reason and analysis to the planning of short-term and contingent actions in the light of our regulative ideals, judging their effectiveness, perhaps, in terms of how their consequences help us to aspire towards our ideals. Thus to pragmatists, all actions may be imperfect, but imperfect actions are generally to be preferred to principled inactivity, and the process of arriving at such partial ways forward has its own kind of beauty.

Literacy then, like truth, is always contextual. Levels of literacy might be judged in contrasting ways: one might have an effective, though unsophisticated, command over a range of discourses, or might take a studiedly literary stance against all forms of new communications technology, for example. Conditions will determine evaluation.

---

[7] E.g. *Republic* Book 10.

[8] *Republic* ed. Lee, pp. 315–320. The democratic character is prone to weakness; what is right is not always popular.

[9] (1998) *Truth and Progress*, Cambridge: Cambridge University Press, p. 2.

Our conception of literacy is bound, therefore, to be double-edged. On the one hand, to be literate is to be able to read and write (or to decode and encode sign systems, for immediate, and often highly functional, purposes); on the other, it is to be valued in a world that values literacy. The pragmatism argued for here merely acknowledges the viability of each of these perspectives, and the tensions that are bound to exist between them, which will never be fully resolvable. It is a liberal, even transcendental pragmatism, which accepts society's need to value some things above others while also recognising the transience and historical situatedness of our educational aspirations, plans, policies and practices. Furthermore, the pragmatic approach to 'literacies' which will be developed here has, I believe, potential use as a framework for curriculum planning, across all disciplines, that allows both for a degree of prescription and for student empowerment: in short, for accountability without constriction.

The impermanence referred to in the penultimate sentence above is nowhere more apparent than in the debate about literacy, where there is a fundamental bifurcation in the assumed scope of the term according to which of two currently powerful sets of theoretical assumptions are adopted. One of these sets of assumptions defines language in terms of speech and writing, while the other works from the premise that languages are sign systems to the conclusion that everything can be regarded as language. We might refer to the former as a purely linguistic tradition; to the latter as a semiotic tradition. Twentieth century thought has been influenced by each of these, with the 'linguistic turn' in philosophy and social theory influenced by philosophers of the analytic school and others in language *qua* language (or language as the 'house of Being', in the terms of Heidegger's *Letter on Humanism*, or the purveyor of logical propositions, to the analytic philosophers[10]), and partly from the structuralism, and subsequently poststructuralism, arising from the appreciation of language as signs and developed largely through disciplines such as sociology and anthropology.[11]

Both traditions, but particularly the latter, are powerfully indebted to the Swiss linguist, Ferdinand de Saussure. Saussure came to find traditional grammatical analysis inadequate to the understanding of language, and postulated that languages were socially constructed systems of signs, used endlessly creatively at the level of utterance ('parole'), yet obeying rules of structure beneath the surface ('langue').[12] Many great linguists of the last century have accepted Saussure's surface-depth distinction without making

---

[10] Wittengenstein's early work is in this tradition: *Tractatus Logico-Philosophicus*, London: Routledge (1974: trans. D.F. Pears and B.F. McGuinness).

[11] See, for example, Lévi-Strauss, C. (1962/1977) *Structural Anthropology*, Harmondsworth: Penguin.

[12] Culler, J. (1976) *Saussure*, London: Fontana.

the radical break between grammatical analysis and 'semiology' (the science of signs, later generally redefined as 'semiotics' after Peirce)[13] for which Saussure argued. Chomsky, for example, distinguished between the 'deep' and 'surface' structure of sentences, yet continued to analyze utterances in terms of sentences, clauses, phrases and word classes ('parts of speech').[14] In this tradition, language has remained something that happens in words, and literacy is about reading and writing.

Ironically, many of those who have really developed Saussure's semiotic project stand outside conventional linguistics altogether. The whole movement of structuralism (and, by extension, poststructuralism) is indebted to Saussure. To understand all social and cultural practice as encoded is to invite the view that everything can be seen as discourse, in which 'language games' and 'forms of life' are inseparable. Wittgenstein's idea of the language game is readily acceptable as referring to all kinds of signifying structures;[15] indeed, an example will be cited below of its application to mathematics education.

It is in the semiotic tradition (often unconsciously, it would seem) that the proliferation of 'literacies' in the educational debate has occurred. Nevertheless, in both traditions, literacies are conditional: in the first (the purely linguistic) because of the diversity of language systems (for example, words may not be susceptible to direct translation), and in the second (the semiotic) because the term can be applied in an apparently infinite range of contexts (so everything becomes 'language'). Educators must work with this conditionality. Pragmatic educators will acknowledge its inevitability. More precisely, they will accept the diversity of linguistic practice and definitions of literacy, the cultural dominance of certain forms of literacy, the unpredictability of the future, and therefore of its demands concerning literacy, and, as a corollary to this, perhaps, the individualization of risk in an increasingly global society in which the network replaces the traditional social and cultural group, and they will plan on the basis of this acceptance. Needless to say, in a society reliant on networking, communication skills become all-important.

Such an acceptance by no means implies an uncritical, non-judgmental relativism, however. Literacy is commonly conceived of not only in terms of its scope, but also in terms of its levels or degrees, and a pragmatic educational policy should accept this. Rates of national literacy are quoted

---

[13] Wiener, P.P. (ed.) (1958) *Charles S. Peirce: selected writings (Values in a Universe of Chance)*, New York: Dover .

[14] Chomsky, N. (1965) *Aspects of the Theory of Syntax*, Cambridge, Mass.: MIT Press.

[15] This is not to imply that Wittgenstein was a structuralist or direct forerunner of structuralism.

glibly in the mass media and accepted easily by public and politicians, though the basis for such figures is always questionable. That they tend to refer to some measure of functional literacy (the ability to cope with reading and writing to an acceptable minimal level) is clear, but that such a measurement is problematized by changes in historical expectation and by arbitrary decisions of analysis is rarely acknowledged: for example, how literate did a farm worker have to be in nineteenth century rural England? How illiterate is 'illiterate' as measured on a test score? Difficulty of measurement is exacerbated by a variety of emphases in both problem definition and data analysis. High profile studies of literacy levels quoted in the popular press tend to focus on levels of functional literacy,[16] despite the more overt emphasis in the United States on cultural literacy since the 1980s to complement this (in other words, understanding the significance of lexical items, such as 'Thanksgiving', within the culture; some might also read an increased UK government interest in this in the emphasis on literary heritage in revisions to the English National Curriculum[17]). Meanwhile, radical educators, influenced by Habermas's conception of critical-emancipatory knowledge,[18] have been more preoccupied with notions of critical literacy, the measurement of which is even more problematic. Henry Giroux, for example, has examined in some depth the potential for critical emancipation through schooling.[19] In the socially critical tradition, to which Habermas, Giroux and Freire can be held to belong, critical literacy implies the ability to 'read' sociocultural practice and attempts at hegemony through the study of texts, thus allowing readers to gain some control over the ideologies and sociocultural practices they thus uncover.

Educational conceptions of literacy therefore exist on two dimensions: one spanning from a narrow view of literacy as words-related to a broad, semiotic view incorporating notions such as emotional, social, scientific and environmental literacies; the other from a purely instrumental, functional view to an idealistic conception of literacy: for example, for emancipation, or as the essence of the civilised. Arguments can be made for all conceivable

---

[16] (In fact, I am not aware of any that have done other than this.)

[17] Hirsch, E.D. (1987) *Cultural Literacy: what every American needs to know*, Boston: Houghton Mifflin.

[18] Habermas, J. (1972) *Knowledge and Human Interests*, Boston: Beacon. Habermas distinguishes between technical-instrumental rationality (knowledge for control derived from and productive of the technological application of science), practical knowledge and critical-emancipatory knowledge, whereby people are able to affect change through recognition of ideological forces at work in their lives.

[19] Giroux, H.A. (1989) *Schooling for Democracy: critical pedagogy in the modern age*, London: Routledge.

combinations of these positions, so education must cater, to some degree, for all of them. We shall now consider the implications of this for practice.

As far as the former dimension is concerned, a pragmatic approach might acknowledge the consensual view that 'literacy', at the moment, is centrally about reading and writing, and that the development of these has a foundational role in education. At the same time, thinking developed from Saussure allows us validly to use 'literacy', if we are prepared to accept it as broadly analogous to 'semiotics', in a seemingly endless range of collocations, from 'computer literacy' to 'emotional literacy'. It can also be argued, however, that the validity of 'literacy' in these collocations depends on the user's understanding of its semiotic connotation, whereas it has often been used relatively indiscriminately in much of the literature, with no such consideration of such validity. 'Literacy' must be one of the most heavily borrowed, yet most indiscriminately interpreted, items in the educational lexicon. However, where the adoption of 'literacy' in this kind of collocation ('computer literacy', 'scientific literacy', 'emotional literacy' and so on) is argued with respect to its theoretical base, it has important ramifications for educational programmes.

A lay consensus may also exist regarding the other dimension of literacy: that to be literate is to have functional, and perhaps cultural, literacy. In its dialogic relations with the rest of society, formal education must acknowledge and respond to this; to do less would be irresponsible. However, there is also evidence that the world of employment, and not merely that of radical educationalists, values the development of skills of initiative, problem-solving and creativity, which can be associated with notions of critical literacy. Education should, therefore, also strive to develop these. It is when we combine the commitment to both functional and critical literacies with the acceptance of 'literacy' as a valid term across the curriculum that the most interesting educational possibilities arise.

It is also important to note at this point that a view of human living as a continuous process of semiotic engagement precludes the necessity for any separate consideration of 'action'. Initial reactions to the thesis developed here often take the view that understanding is useless if it does not promote action in the world. A view of living as 'reading and writing the world' incorporates action, however. The taking of action is both implicit and inevitable in the development of disciplined literacies.

On this basis, let us assume that there is validity in the application of 'literacy' to spheres of human activity beyond reading and writing. What might it mean to be functionally, culturally and critically literate in areas as diverse as information and communications technology (ICT), mathematics and environmental education?

In terms of ICT, any definition of functional literacy must embrace the user's capacity to manipulate the hardware: to locate switches and use keyboard and mouse. Beyond that, we might apply Williams and Snipper's notion of functional literacy as operating 'at some minimal level', where this minimum is defined contextually.[20] In other words, the functionally literate computer-user can carry out required tasks, as set by either employer or by domestic or other circumstance, without using the computer creatively or with initiative. The latter abilities, amounting to the capacity to use computers for self- or community-empowerment, might be seen as the marks of the critically literate computer user. As far as cultural computer literacy is concerned, issues arise in relation to the role of computers in the culture (for *what* they are, or should be, used) and in relation to their use by those enjoying high cultural capital (*how* they should be used: email etiquette and so on).

Functional mathematical literacy might be defined as the ability to cope mathematically: to undertake simple mathematical calculations required in daily life: largely, to be numerate. However, an important philosophical question concerning mathematics renders any more complex consideration of the issue problematic. This question concerns the relationship of mathematics to the external world, and has been raised in a recent paper by Yvette Solomon. Solomon, citing Wittgenstein, argues that maths is essentially a language game undertaken within a community of practice and only understandable in its own terms, and is thus not prey to the 'procedural' versus 'principled' understanding debate associated with Edwards and Mercer.[21] The variation in perspectives on this issue clearly has potentially profound consequences for mathematics education. If maths can only be 'understood' in relation to other experience, then functional mathematical literacy becomes the ability to 'do' maths but not understand it, while critical mathematical literacy might imply the ability to generate new mathematical understanding from one's environment. Conversely, if maths is a language game (i.e. a form of truth in itself), then functional mathematical literacy can be seen as the ability to 'cope' mathematically, and critical mathematical literacy as the ability to use maths creatively. In either case, it might be argued that cultural literacy is a relatively redundant concept in relation to mathematics education, unless cultural perspectives on the history, uses and applications of mathematics are considered.

The application of the functional/cultural/critical tripartite literacy model to environmental education will be explored in some depth in the following

---

[20] See, for example, Williams, J.D. and Snipper, G.C. (1990) *Literacy and Bilingualism*, New York: Longman.

[21] Edwards, D. and Mercer, N. (1987) *Common Knowledge: the development of understanding in the classroom*, London: Routledge; Solomon, Y. (1998) Teaching Mathematics: ritual, principle and practice, *Journal of Philosophy of Education* 32/3, 377–390.

chapter. As a brief introduction to the key ideas, functional *environmental literacy* might be taken to refer to the ability to recognize and name something in the natural environment: for example, a certain species of bird; furthermore, perhaps, to recognise several birds within a particular habitat, and to know which are birds of prey, which are summer visitors and so on: in other words, the ability to make 'literal' sense of surroundings in the light of more abstract forms of classification, just as we make sense of words on a page.

Cultural environmental literacy might include the ability to understand the significance that society attaches to certain kinds of environment (such as national parks, or even grass verges), and to what might be referred to as environmental icons. Such icons include, of course, living natural objects, from mountains to trees (Table Mountain in South Africa, for example). Cultural environmental literacy would be required to understand the role of farmland in the culture of the highly populated South-East of England, or ancient national forests throughout the World.

Critical environmental literacy implies the power to develop an understanding of the factors that contribute to environmental change and to have a view on how to further or oppose that change in a way, which can be translated, into action. As signalled above, if we take the notion of environment as text seriously enough, it can be argued that our relations with nature are essentially a matter of semiotic engagement, and that critical environmental literacy can thus embrace, or replace, the notions of 'action competence' that have been seen as important outcomes of environmental education, rather than merely supplementing them: that we 'write' as well as 'read' our environments.[22] Critical environmental literacy might therefore involve the ability to explore questions such as 'What does [a place or an issue] mean to me?'; 'What does it mean to us, or to others?'; 'What are the consequences of carrying on in this way [in relation to this place or this issue]?'; 'Should we act differently, and if so how, and what will the consequences of such action be?'; 'How do we translate our values into effective action – and are our values themselves ready for change as a result of what we now know or feel?'

Accepting some essential differences between the discourses of ICT, mathematics and environmental education discussed above, the use of 'literacy', *qua* semiotics, as an umbrella term can be particularly useful in curriculum planning. Indeed, insofar as the curriculum comprises, reflects and adapts distinct 'language games', traditional notions of cross-curricularity are problematized (knowledge does not come in 'topics' so

---

[22] For a discussion of action competence, see Jensen, B.B. and Schnack, K. (1997) The Action Competence Approach in Environmental Education, *Environmental Education Research* 3/2, 163–178.

much as in ways of knowing), and an adherence to 'literacies' along the functional-critical dimension may seem a more valid framework for curriculum planning. The 'areas of experience' model derived from the work of Paul Hirst and heavily influential in British curriculum planning in the 1970s and '80s still offers an alternative, of course, but remains less sensitive to the idea of disciplines as discrete discourses. Hirst and Peters were clearly much influenced by the language game but seemed to retain some concern to make the curriculum as a whole 'add up', and thus, arguably, effectively distorted Wittgenstein by making the language game answerable to something greater than itself. At the very least, Hirst and Peters were widely interpreted as providing a blueprint for a 'broad and balanced' curriculum. The potential emphasis on separate literacies was thus lost.[23]

The pragmatic model proposed here does not require the curriculum to make sense as a whole, yet it does allow for curriculum planning. A further advantage of such a 'literacies' approach to curriculum planning might be that it enshrines a commitment to both 'core' learning, at the functional and cultural levels, and to freedom of thought and action, at the critical level. In other words, it is possible to reach some agreement concerning what amounts to functional literacy in any one context, as well as on which subjects might be allotted curriculum time, thus allowing for specification of a minimum educational entitlement, to which providers can be held accountable; yet, at the same time, the curriculum must also encourage critical questioning and creativity, neither of which can be prescribed, in order for critical literacy to develop. A further advantage is that it focuses curriculum planners in each subject area to consider the relative emphases they wish to place on functional, cultural and critical literacies.

Educational planning always involves some degree of prescription. Pragmatic educators who acknowledge the conditionality of literacies must also acknowledge the imperative to make decisions about the curriculum. A relatively sustainable framework (i.e. one that seems so now, as nothing is absolutely sustainable) is needed for this because of our awareness of the uncertainty of the foreseeable future, in which claims for cultural pluralism will continue to oppose equally inevitable efforts at cultural dominance: a situation interpreted by commentators such as Giddens and Castells as the increasing globalization of economy and society continuing to result in the increased individualization of risk, and in the replacement of stable communities by contingent networks. As noted above, in a world of networks rather than stable communities, the necessity is increased for individuals to engage themselves in effective communication with others, a

---

[23] Hirst, P. (1974) *Knowledge and the Curriculum*, London: Routledge and Kegan Paul.

prerequisite of which is the level and scope of literacy that make such communication possible.

With respect to this, 'literacy' has the potential to remain a very useful notion in educational planning, but only when used in a disciplined way. It must be 'disciplined' in two respects: firstly, requiring that those who refer to literacy are rigorous in their application of the term; and secondly, in relation to acknowledging curricular disciplines as discourses in their own terms, so that functional historical literacy and functional scientific literacy remain distinct, for example. Strictly, perhaps, to remain true to the spirit of the argument hitherto, we should speak of the development of an educational semiotics rather than of literacies; however, while we have no notion of the 'semiotic', as opposed to the 'literate', individual, we are constrained, pragmatically, to pursue literacy as our main educational goal.

In the next chapter, I consider the degree to which policy has succeeded in adopting a broad view of literacies, such as that outlined above, using the example of environmental education in England and Wales.

Chapter 7

Environmental Literacy: functional, cultural, critical. The case of the SCAA guidelines

This chapter further explores the implications of curriculum development as 'literacies' with respect to environmental education/ education for sustainable development, critiquing government guidelines in England and Wales for narrow curricular responses to lofty aspirations in this area.[1]

As discussed in the previous chapter, the tripartite division of literacy skills as *functional*, *cultural* and *critical* can be useful in both planning and evaluating programmes of environmental education. As exemplification of the latter, the model is applied to a brief discussion of the School Curriculum and Assessment Authority (SCAA) guidelines for environmental education in England produced in 1996.[2] It is concluded that these offer opportunities for teachers to develop all three kinds of environmental literacy, but with an emphasis on skills development that must be seen as largely functional.

---

[1] Permission has been granted by Carfax Publishing to reproduce material in this chapter from Stables, A. (1998) Environmental Literacy: functional, cultural, critical. The case of the SCAA guidelines, *Environmental Education Research* 4/ 2, 155–164. See also the publisher's website at http://www.tandf.co.uk.

[2] These are the most recently produced national guidelines for teachers in England and Wales specifically relating to environmental education, even though SCAA has since been superseded by the QCA (Qualifications and Curriculum Authority). In 2002, guidance for teaching sustainable development issues appeared on the National Curriculum website at www.nc.uk.net/esd. However, education for sustainable development (ESD), thus defined, is only partly concerned with environmental issues. The Web guidance is less detailed than that critiqued here, but retains the same emphasis in terms of curriculum mapping, insofar as ESD is seen as principally the domain of geography and science (along with citizenship, a new subject for England and Wales since 1996) though also relevant to literacy and numeracy. These guidelines are not sufficiently detailed to sustain the level of critique offered of the earlier specifications in this chapter, though there is no obvious evidence that the criticisms offered here have been addressed in the sustainable development guidelines.

Thus the response of curriculum planners can be seen as falling short of policy aspirations.

The term 'environmental literacy' has been used hitherto in the environmental education literature, but while it has been given working definitions, these have not been derived directly from a systematic engagement with literacy debates within language and literature studies. As part of the American work on 'standards', Roth, in 1992, provided a framework for environmental literacy with relation to knowledge, affect, skills and behaviour at three levels of competence (nominal, functional and operational).[3] For UNESCO, at about the same time, Marcinkowski provided a set of nine statements which amount to what environmental literacy might be taken to be, relating to knowledge, understanding, attitudes and active involvement.[4] In Scotland, curriculum planners have included environmental literacy as one of the four goals of 'environmental citizenship', defining it in terms of 'knowledge and understanding of the components of the system'.[5] While each of these definitions of environmental literacy might have its practical uses, none is overtly grounded in the primary academic debate about the nature of literacy.

In essence, the case for regarding environmental education as the development of a kind (or of certain kinds) of literacy is an easy one to make: the environment is moulded by human hands, is susceptible to action predetermined by human value systems and cultural norms and is, therefore, appropriately studied using approaches derived from the arts and humanities as well as from the sciences. This simple argument can be elaborated in a number of ways.

First, work in a number of disciplines in recent years has tended to give increased emphasis to the role of humanity is shaping the natural environment. To give two examples, Simon Schama explains how areas of assumed wilderness have been shaped by human culture over a millennium.[6] Bill McKibben went further in 1990 claiming, more controversially, that no natural event or place on Earth is free from human intervention.[7] In terms of environmental issues, it would be impossible to conduct effective debate

---

3   Roth, C. (1992) *Environmental Literacy: its roots, evolution and direction in the 1990s*, Ohio: Ohio State University.
4   Marcinkowski, T. (1991) The Relationship Between Environmental Literacy and Responsible Environmental Behavior in Environmental Education, in Maldague, M. (ed.) *Methods and Techniques for Evaluating Environmental Education*, Paris: UNESCO.
5   Scottish Office (1993) *National Strategy for Environmental Education in Scotland*, Edinburgh: HMSO.
6   Schama, S. (1995) *Landscape and Memory*, New York: Random House.
7   McKibben, B (1990) *The End of Nature*, Harmondsworth: Penguin.

about road building, the European Common Agricultural Policy, mineral extraction or global warming without considerable attention to ideology and human motive.

Second, as discussed in the previous chapter, the disciplines associated with the study of language have seen their scope broadened throughout the twentieth century, so that terms such as 'language', 'text' and 'discourse' have been open to broader interpretation than in the eighteenth and nineteenth centuries, and language has increasingly been seen not just as the vehicle of ideas, but as the subject of philosophy and social theory in its own right.

Finally, in fields other than education, links have already been drawn between the language arts and environmental studies. The author attended the first British conference on Literature and the Natural Environment, at the University of Wales, Swansea in 1997. Such conferences began in the early 1990s in the United States, where a journal (Interdisciplinary Studies in Literature and Environment) exists to develop the field. There are already some significant works of ecocriticism.[8] Environmental philosophy, originally known as ecosophy, has a related, much longer history.

It is clear from the above that there are a number of justifications for considering the development of environmental awareness and agency in relation to the development of our reading, linguistic and cultural awareness and skills. It is the purpose of the remainder of this chapter to show what this means in practice, and to evaluate a key environmental education policy document in England and Wales in terms of the degree to which it promotes the development of functional, cultural and critical environmental literacies.

There follows a rather fuller account of these than appeared in the previous chapter.

Functional Environmental Literacy

Functional print literacy is the ability to decode what is encoded within the black marks on the white paper into intelligible words, phrases and clauses, and to understand their literal meaning on a superficial level. Functional literacy, for example, allows you to read a sign bearing an instruction, such as 'Stop!' and to act upon it. It allows you to read a story but does not account for whether you can draw any implications from it. Functional literacy (with relation to print) can therefore be taught through the learning

---

[8] E.g. Bate, J. (1991) *Romantic Ecology: Wordsworth and the environmental tradition*, London: Routledge; Buell, L. (1995) *The Environmental Imagination: Thoreau, nature writing and the formation of American culture*, Cambridge, Mass.: Belknap Press of Harvard University Press; Coupe, L. (2000) *The Green Studies Reader: from Romanticism to ecocriticism*, London: Routledge.

of phonic rules. It is not directly concerned with reading for meaning. However, it does involve the ability to recognise the surface meaning of words and phrases in context: for instance, to understand 'stop' in constructions such as 'pull out the organ stop', 'forgot to use a full stop' and 'Danger – Stop!' Statistics concerning rates of literacy and illiteracy generally relate to functional literacy, and obscure the fact that what it takes to be functionally literate varies considerably from time to time and place to place. (Consider, for example, the level of print literacy needed to 'function' as a farm worker in the nineteenth century and as a computer operator in the twentieth.)

Functional print literacy can be measured by objective tests, which can be purely summative, or may be diagnostic if subjected to miscue analysis, which analyses readers' errors. Functional literacy is not just a matter of knowing what words mean, but of being able to *find out* what they mean in the context of whole sentences by the use of phonic and contextual cues. Functional literacy also involves being able to read words referring to commonplace abstractions (beauty, goodness, fear etc.). It involves literal comprehension.

Functional environmental literacy must, therefore, refer not only to the ability to remember what an oak tree is, but to recognize one; not only to recognize several trees within a given area, but to know whether they form part of a wood or an area of parkland. Functional environmental literacy must also involve the ability to ascertain, from contextual cues, what something half known is likely to be: for instance, to make an informed guess, using observation, at the types of woodland flower within a beech copse overlying chalk rather than an oak wood on more acid soil. Functional literacy is not, therefore, a mere prerequisite to more advanced forms of literacy, but involves a series of complex skills and an accumulation of knowledge which has unlimited capacity for growth. Arguably, much science education in schools focuses chiefly on what is defined here as functional literacy, whether or not this entirely reflects intentions. Certainly, its role in environmental education should not be underestimated.

Both cultural and critical literacy are impossible without functional literacy. Just as the ability to decode print is a prerequisite to the development of deeper levels of comprehension of the passage to be read, so is knowledge of the natural world a condition of the development of awareness of environmental issues and of the ability to take effective action.

However, functional environmental literacy is not enough because it does not, of itself, engage the learner (though many learners may already be highly motivated), and it does not engage either with the crucial notion of what the environment *means*, either to others or to the learner. Effective environmental education, therefore, can never abandon its scientific knowledge base, but must always move beyond it, so that scientific knowledge is used to inform what are essentially human value judgments. In terms of environmental literacy, we must acknowledge the importance of the functional but place it alongside the cultural, and see both as conditions of the critical, as only critical environmental literacy can facilitate effective environmental action.

Cultural Environmental Literacy

Although C.A. Bowers used the term 'cultural literacy' with reference to cross-cultural issues in the early 1970s, the work of E.D. Hirsch has had a much greater and more recent effect on literacy teaching in the United States and has enjoyed a considerable influence elsewhere, not least because of the author's closeness to the Reagan administration.[9] (J.S. Simmons has given a fascinating account of the development of the U.S. literacy curriculum during the 1980s, with particular reference to this issue.[10]) Hirsch's cultural literacy relates to understanding of the dominant culture rather than increased sensitivity to minorities. Hirsch actually produced a list of 'what every American needs to know', on the assumption that social and cultural cohesion depends on the ability to understand the significance American society places on, for example, Thanksgiving; not merely its existence as, say, a public holiday. Like functional literacy, cultural literacy is, in a sense, passive: it is the ability to know the received wisdom about some cultural event or institution rather than to make meaning for yourself. However, it is a powerful idea, the ramifications of which can be seen in the various ways in which governments around the world have begun, or continued, to use national curricula to reinforce national identities.

Cultural literacy refers to the ability to understand the significance that society attaches to cultural icons. Such icons include, of course, living natural objects: national parks; the Californian redwood; the English oak. An increased cultural environmental literacy would be gained by a reading of Schama's *Landscape and Memory*, in which the author discusses a series of landscapes of rich significance to contemporary societies (including part of the Eastern European forest, the English Greenwood and the Californian redwoods) in terms of cultural history with respect to the ways in which these landscapes have been viewed, used and reshaped over a millennium.[11]

---

[9] Hirsch, E.D. (1987) *Cultural Literacy: what every American needs to know*, Boston: Houghton Mifflin; Bowers, C.A. (1974) *Cultural Literacy for Freedom: an existential perspective on teaching, curriculum and school policy*, Eugene, Or.: Elan.

[10] In Marum, E. (ed.) (1996) *Children and Books in the Modern World*, London: Falmer.

[11] See Note 6.

One of the abiding impressions gained from a reading of *Landscape and Memory* is that the landscapes in question have often been strongly shaped by cultural and social forces throughout the period in question. Schama effectively dispels the still partly-held misconception, for example, that much of England was covered with virgin forest until the last couple of hundred years.

On one level, a degree of cultural environmental literacy merely enables one to recognise the significance of natural images in human culture, along with some recognition of why and to whom they are significant: the American bald eagle, or the white dove of peace, for example. However, it also allows for an understanding of why the landscape itself is as it is, shaped not merely by climate, glaciation and topography, but by arguments about enclosure, the need for timber and patterns of land ownership dating back many centuries. While functional environmental literacy develops knowledge of what natural things are, cultural environmental literacy thus enables us to explain why they are there when the causes are clearly not simply geological or climatic with no apparent human intervention.

Cultural literacy depends on a degree of acceptance of cultural hegemony: it links the learner with a dominant value system. The culturally literate individual in England will know what is implied by the term 'heart of oak', or understand the English Lake District as a kind of symbol of Wordsworthian Romanticism, even though these conceptions may be more associated with English 'high culture' than with popular culture, as well as having no scientific basis. Cultural literacy refers more to cultural heritage than to cultural analysis. The subtitle of Hirsch's book is 'What every American needs to know'. Insofar as cultural literacy is empowering, it empowers by giving the learner access to socially powerful perspectives; cultural literacy alone does not enable the learner to act upon that knowledge, once acquired. Effective action requires critical literacy.

Critical Environmental Literacy

Critical literacy implies the ability to make sense in your own terms of the ideational potential of a text. It includes the ability to 'get behind' the text to interpret it in terms of its ideological underpinnings: to distinguish, for example, between factual account, polemic and propaganda. 'Critical' here is used in a double sense. On the one hand it has a long pedigree in the liberal-humanist tradition of literary criticism in which the 'critical appreciation' of texts demanded an extended personal response and evaluation of the text as work of art: an exploration of the reader's initial affective response. On the other hand, it can refer to Habermas's conception of 'critical-emancipatory' knowledge, whereby the reader responds to the text not merely as a naive individual who can only interpret for practical ends, but as one who *understands* the cultural, social and political forces that shape the text, and can therefore guard against being taken in by it, and thus effect change at a deeper level. Because of this dual use of the term 'critical' (the personally engaged and the socially critical), late twentieth century readings of texts have varied from the overtly personal to the apparently dispassionate and deliberately political: Marxist readings, feminist readings, ecofeminist readings and so on. Although in general, this book promotes a highly interpretive view of education, for the purposes of this chapter, 'critical literacy' will be held to relate to both liberal-humanist and the socially critical perspectives: i.e. to that kind of literacy which involves active exploration of significance and meaning, whatever one's views on the potential objectivity of such exploration.

Critical literacy is the ability to understand the text on a deeper and more creative level: the ability to discuss the use of genre in context, to question the motives and ideology of the text, and to explore and develop personal (and broader social) response to it. Critical environmental literacy must then imply the power to develop an understanding of the factors that contribute to environmental change and to have a view on how to further to oppose that change in a way that can be translated into action. Critical environmental literacy involves the ability to explore the questions cited in the previous chapter.[12]

As has been stressed above, critical literacy cannot be effectively developed without good levels of both functional and cultural literacy, though the latter are arguably pointless without the former. Critical environmental literacy relies on functional environmental literacy because both environmental debate and environmental action rely on information. Critical environmental literacy relies on cultural literacy not simply because environmental debate and action need to be grounded in an awareness of the norms and values of, say, national cultures, but because influence on environmental change demands an understanding of the norms and values of the *dominant* culture.

A possible objection to the model might be that, while it may be possible to apply this model to environmental education, it is of limited value so to do, since environmental problems require scientific analysis and scientifically based solutions.

In response to this, there is no doubt that environmental education could not operate effectively purely as an arts or humanities subject. However, all environmental issues are essentially either human issues or issues viewed from a human perspective. Many of the key terms of the environmental debate, including 'balance' and 'sustainability' are terms relating to human

---

[12] Scottish Office (1993) *National Strategy for Environmental Education in Scotland*, Edinburgh: HMSO, p. 64.

values. Science must inform our choices but they cannot be made without reference to ethical, and often aesthetic, considerations. Thus, while each discipline can develop its own form of environmental literacy,[13] the arts and humanities, or 'cultural studies', should certainly play their role in informing decisions about environmental action.

Specifically, the contribution of the 'environmental literacy' approach might be greatest in the following areas:

i)   In understanding how, and why, approaches to the environment have changed and developed over time;
ii) In ensuring that choices about environmental action take into account ethical and aesthetic, as well as scientific considerations with respect to their likely consequences (i.e. to consider the question, 'What will this actually *mean* for us/others/nature?').

As we shall see below, English National Curriculum guidelines developed in the late 1990s were intended to prepare students to make responsible, and not merely informed, choices for a sustainable future. However, a limited view of environmental literacy limits the scope and ambition of the guidelines.

Environmental Literacies and the 1996 SCAA Guidelines

What follows is not intended as a detailed, still less a hostile critique, since the SCAA guidelines offer many examples of noteworthy practice to teachers and schools determined to pursue an aspect of the curriculum which is given very little weighting in the UK in terms of school inspection and accountability. The purpose is merely to show how the model can be applied to the evaluation of a curriculum policy document by reference to some

---

[13] Stables, A. and Scott, W. (2001) Disciplined Environmental Literacies, *Environmental Education* 68, 14–16. See also Bishop, K., Reid, A., Stables, A., Lencastre, M., Stoer, S. and Soetaert, R. (2000) Developing Environmental Awareness Through Literature and Media Education: curriculum development in the context of teachers' practice, *Canadian Journal of Environmental Education* 5, 268–286. Here, the authors report on a European Commission funded project in which development work in literature and media education was undertaken with reference to five interpretations of the concept 'environmental text': literary texts with environmental themes, non-fictional texts about the environment, students' own texts related to the environment, responding to aspects of the environment as text, and recreating the environment with reference to aesthetic and other textual criteria.

isolated, but hopefully representative, examples from the text. Although there has been more recent advice to the British government on sustainability and environment within the curriculum, the SCAA guidelines had not been formally superseded by 2002.[14]

The document opens with some quotations from important government sources: the Secretary of State for Education and Employment, the Secretary of State for the Environment, and a 'British Government Panel on Sustainable Development'.

What is particularly interesting about these initial quotations is the emphasis the government ministers put on what is defined above as critical environmental literacy.

Gillian Shephard (UK Government): 'We need to be aware, as individuals, of how our own choices about a myriad of everyday things can influence the quality of life....choices with a real relevance to school pupils....They will have to understand just how great or how small are the risks of environmental change associated with different policies.'

John Gummer (UK Government): '..And sustainable development pressures on these young people will not go away. We need to involve them in the issues now, and help them gain ownership of some of the solutions' (SCAA, 1996: Foreword).

This emphasis is retained in the Aims of the Guidelines, particularly in Aims 2 and 3:

(2) 'encourage pupils to examine and interpret the environment from a variety of perspectives – physical, geographical, biological, sociological, economic, political, technological, historical, aesthetic, ethical and spiritual;'
(3) 'arouse pupils' awareness and curiosity about the environment and encourage active participation in resolving environmental problems.'

What is interesting in the body of the document as a whole is that this emphasis on critical environmental literacy is not maintained. The overall weighting of the exemplar materials that comprise the bulk of the document is on functional environmental literacy. Similarly, arts and humanities subjects, excluding geography, are not given the same weighting as scientific and technical subjects, excluding geography. Each example specifies, in bold print, the subject areas to which it contributes. A crude count reveals the overall numbers as follows: arts/humanities (excl. geog.): 16 (including several references to English because the activity involves

---

[14] SCAA (School Curriculum and Assessment Authority [UK]) (1996) *Teaching Environmental Matters through the National Curriculum*, London: HMSO. See Note 2.

the practising of English skills); mathematics/science/technical subjects (excl.geog.): 39. This bias is neither necessarily conscious nor does it detract from the usefulness of the exemplar materials; however, it does reflect an assumed emphasis within environmental education programmes. Alongside this, the exemplar materials do not place the same emphasis on the development of critical (or cultural) environmental literacy that the ministerial statements would seem to have urged. Indeed, the balance of the Aims (quoted in part above) is not reflected elsewhere in the documentation. The 'Management Issues' section, for example, does not really expand on the critical elements within the Aims, but instead concentrates on generic features of good curriculum planning, on auditing (but not really evaluating the 'critical' element) and on locating sources of further information. Throughout the document, the term 'education about the environment' is used for the sake of ease (though there is a full explication of this towards the beginning), and this might be seen as encouraging functional and cultural, rather than critical, environmental literacy.

It is beyond the scope of this book to undertake a detailed analysis of the exemplar materials. They embody, as has been stated, excellent environmental education practice, and have doubtless proved of considerable use to teachers. While they cover all aspects of environmental literacy, they do not, however, place the same emphasis on the critical that might be expected from the opening of the document. At one point, a figure shows how the subject departments of a particular school identified the relevant areas of their own subject orders to the teaching of EE. Here the emphasis is *entirely* on the functional. Even the inclusions from English ('writing for a range of purposes and audiences' and 'developing pupils' ability to write poetry') seem to be mechanistic, and to avoid consideration of the ethical, the culturally historical or the aesthetic. Indeed, it is arguably in the subject orders of the National Curriculum themselves (relevant sections of which are quoted in the SCAA document) that the genesis of this emphasis on the functional lies. Here there is very little emphasis on either the cultural or the critical, though the examination requirements for Religious Education (not National Curriculum orders in the strict sense, but quoted in the Guidelines *in lieu*) contain potentially challenging objectives in this respect, including 'learning about Jewish teaching on *tikkum olam* (mending the world) and how this affects contemporary Jewish attitudes towards green issues' and 'identify and promote exploration of, and reflection upon, questions about the meaning and purpose of life'. Little in the Geography orders, by contrast, seems designed to promote either cultural or critical environmental literacy: an exception is 'considering the issues that arise from people's interaction with their environment'.

As previously stated, the above comments on the SCAA Guidelines do not aspire to a full analysis. The intention is merely to show that the threefold classification of environmental literacy into functional, cultural and critical can be of use in evaluating, and thus reformulating, environmental education syllabuses and courses. Specifically, in this case, the question is raised as to whether government ministers' intentions to promote critical environmental literacy are reflected in the curriculum guidelines and statutory orders for which they are effectively responsible. The argument remains that the roles of the aesthetic, the ethical and the cultural continue to be underplayed within environmental education, and that considering environmental education, or education for sustainable development, in terms of literacies can go some way to redressing this imbalance.

Ecological crisis is cited in Chapter 1 as one of the three great challenges to assumptions in our educational thinking. While the development of environmental literacy (or literacies[15]) can be seen as a practical curricular and pedagogical response to the ecological crisis, questions remain about the degree to which humanity is capable of transcending its own material interests, if that is what is required, to guarantee a sustainable future. There are implications here, however, that go far beyond the question of what should be contained within a curriculum document. If the primary purpose of education is to develop readings of the world, how does this impact on a broader understanding of what constitutes good practice in teaching and learning? The idea of teaching for active exploration and development of personal and social identity is discussed in the penultimate chapter. Meanwhile, it is to the broader issue of the possibility of education for sustainable development that we now turn.

---

[15] Stables and Scott, 2001 – see Note 13.

Chapter 8

Can We Educate for Sustainability?

This chapter considers the approaches to knowledge, understanding and learning that might best serve to promote environmental and ecological sustainability and/or 'sustainable development'. A range of possible epistemological 'takes' on the environment are discussed, and their pedagogical implications explored. It considers the limits of human capacity to understand and, therefore, protect 'nature'.[1]

The project of environmental education/education for sustainable development (ESD) is, to some extent, characterized by paradox. Not only are the key terms of which it tends to be constituted subject to the superfluity and deferral of meaning to which, according to Jacques Derrida and others, all terms are subject (i.e. it is effectively impossible to 'pin down' terms such as Nature and Sustainability), but ESD is also largely a modernist response to a crisis of modernity. As such, it is prey both to ideological forces that were generated without concern for the environment, and to the potential ambivalence of policy terms such as 'sustainable development'.[2] It lacks recognition as a discipline, and finds itself caught between the sometimes incommensurable language games of the physical sciences and the humanities.[3] Furthermore, approaches to ESD can depend on conflicting philosophical and epistemological assumptions that are incompatible in terms of their implications for curriculum. There is not simply one, uncontested, Nature that can be understood in one, uncontested way.

---

[1] Permission has been granted by Carfax Publishing to reproduce material in this chapter from Stables, A. (2001) 'Who Drew the Sky: conflicting assumptions in environmental education', *Educational Philosophy and Theory* 33/2, pp. 245–256.

[2] Stables, A. (1996) 'Paradox in Compound Educational Policy Slogans: evaluating equal opportunities in subject choice', *British Journal of Educational Studies* 44/2, 159–167; there is specific attention to 'sustainable development' as one such paradoxical slogan in Stables, A. and Scott, W. (2002) The Quest for Holism in Environmental Education, *Environmental Education Research* 8/1, 53–60.

[3] For a fuller discussion of this, see Stables, A. (2002) Environmental Education and the Arts/Science Divide: the case for a disciplined environmental literacy, delivered as *ICE (International Centre for the Environment)* seminar, University of Bath, 18th November 1997, and published in Winnett, A. (ed.) *Towards an Environmental Research Agenda*, Vol. II, Basingstoke: Palgrave (2002).

At the same time, ESD seems valueless if it fails to develop some form of environmental ethic. However, given the position of ESD, it may be that this can only feasibly be developed through a critical retrospective on all the major traditions of modernity, conducted through immanent critique of curricular disciplines and attention to the philosophical and cultural assumptions that underpin our practices in relation to the environment.

The modern curriculum, certainly at the intermediate levels of education beyond which many of us do not progress, is still riven by a science-arts/humanities divide, in which issues of objective truth are largely separated from issues of aesthetics and the morality of human action. In this dualistic world, certain questions are simply not appropriate. For example: imagine the sky on a day of 'sunshine and showers'. Across it are etched three or four aeroplane vapour trails, in varying degrees of increasing fragmentation, the tails of the least-recently produced a mass of tiny clouds virtually indistinguishable from those produced by other means. This sky was the result of natural processes in which human beings were implicated, possibly on a number of levels. This sky was, indeed, constructed; it was, in a sense, a text, particularly in the ancient sense of 'text' as 'weaving' (from the Latin 'textere', to weave). As Roland Barthes reminded us in *The Death of the Author* (though referring to literary texts), it is always a moot question as to who was responsible for it.[4] On the other hand, of course (we say as scientists), it was not a text at all.

Although much exciting work in higher education is interdisciplinary, its success depends on specialists coming together rather than on homogeneity of prior experience; the history of modernity is a history of proliferation rather than reduction of forms of knowledge. Post-Darwinian natural science has certainly been characterized by competition between related but distinct disciplines.

In so far as there are at least two ways to make sense of the sky, there is also a variety of ways in which environmental educators can respond to this dualism. Some practice in ESD might assume that to see the sky as art is useful in engaging and encouraging that love of the natural world which can be a motivator for more disciplined scientific study, or that such an engagement can serve the ongoing exploration of 'environmental issues'. Following Kant, we might claim that aesthetic response precedes scientific response.[5] Such an approach has continuing appeal for those educators who will be considered below as of scientific-realist dispositions, since it assumes that a sense of wonder at nature is a fitting prerequisite for the

4   Barthes, R. (1977) 'The Death of the Author', in *Image-Music-Text* (trans. Heath, S.) London: Fontana, 142–148.
5   Kant, I. (trans. Meredith, J.C.) (1978) *The Critique of Judgment*, Oxford: Oxford University Press.

pursuit of natural science. In the *Critique of Judgment*, Kant construed the imagination in terms of the application of the rational to the empirical, and intuition as both cognition and sensibility. In responding to the order of nature (the 'beautiful') or to its transcendent grandeur (the 'sublime'), our subjective conceptualisations are somehow validated (in experience of the beautiful) or exceeded (in experience of the sublime). Thus, in describing the kind of engagement described above as aesthetic, it can be argued that aesthetic response is a good precursor to critical scientific study. Indeed:

'Intuitions are always required to verify the reality of our concepts.'[6]

While Plato could find no place for those who studied what their senses presented to them, lest these were merely the reflected flickerings of the firelight on the walls of the cave in which they sheltered, turning their backs on the potentially blinding light of the outside world,[7] Kant's realism allows us to use our apperceptions to question and refine our *a priori* categories, thus enabling a dialectical relationship to exist between the empirical and the rational.

As contemporary cultures are still bound by a strong commitment to both empiricism and theory, and given Kant's influence in undermining both pure Cartesian (and Platonic) rationalism and thorough-going eighteenth century empiricism, there is much in such a Kantian-inspired view that retains a strong explanatory power for ESD. Furthermore, Kant was an influential figure for the Nineteenth Century Romantics to whom the present day owes much in terms of how the non-human world is understood. However, much twentieth century thinking was inclined to reject Kant's metaphysical baggage, along with other holistic and totalizing views of nature, including those indebted to Hegel. More recent commentators have been less than fully convinced by Kant's account of the distinction between aesthetic and teleological judgment, his arguments about intuition, and his considerations of the sublime and the beautiful.[8] Twentieth century thinkers, in a range of disciplines, have drawn our attention rather to the essential role of language in constituting both ontology and epistemology. Some, such as Lacan, tended to stress the alienating role of language in constituting our subjec-

---

[6] *Ibid.* p. 221.
[7] *Republic* Book VII.
[8] See, for instance, Schaper, E. (1992) 'Taste, Sublimity and Genius: the aesthetics of nature and art', in Guyer, P. (ed.) *The Cambridge Companion to Kant* Cambridge: Cambridge University Press.

tivities in ways which cannot be at one with 'nature',[9] and this view has had obvious appeal for Marxist critical theorists who already accepted the idea of the alienation of work and other human activity under capitalism. (Hence the relationship between socialism and environmentalism that still forms the foundation of much thinking about ESD, and that will be described as 'critical-realist' below.) Others, influenced by the later Wittgenstein, hold that understanding is bound within language games, since language determines human understanding. For some poststructuralists, such as Derrida, Lyotard and Baudrillard, language not only determines us, but renders futile the quest for truth and all our other 'grand narratives', including those of progress and, by implication, nature.[10] The work of Derrida and others stresses that such a quest is undermined by the simple fact that there is no valid metaphysics of presence (an assumption on which Kant depended) and no meaning is fixed: we can only position 'nature', for example, by differentiating it from what it is not; there is nothing essentially 'there'. Less controversially, environmental philosophers such as Kate Soper have reminded us that there is no stable historical agreement about key concepts such as 'nature'.[11]

Since the late 1980s, a further linguistic turn has occurred in social psychology (that some have referred to as a 'second cognitive revolution') with discursive psychologists such as Rom Harré holding not that everything *is* language, but that issues of human identity and perception and of social life are best understood *as if they were* language, rather than through the methods of the natural and mathematical sciences. In other words, what matters is not so much the empirical study of human behaviour as the discursive understanding of social acts and actions, taking full account

---

9   At the risk of oversimplification, the psychoanalyst Lacan's view might be summarised as follows: the self as socialised entity is always at odds with the self as unconscious drives, thus the whole human condition is one of dislocation and alienation. See Lacan, J. (1977) *Écrits: a selection*, New York: Norton.

10 Lyotard, J.-F. (1984) *The Postmodern Condition: a report on knowledge*, Manchester: Manchester University Press. All of Jacques Derrida's work is, in effect, a challenge to the Platonic essentialist assumption that words refer to things with absolute and fixed meanings. Extending the structuralists' assumption that meanings are the product of relationships rather than essences, Derrida goes further to argue that spatial and temporal contexts render any agreement about meaning and the relationship of words to things futile. From a more sociological perspective, Jean Baudrillard's work has proceeded on the assumption that a society geared towards consumption rather than production is a culture in which signs take over from their former referents; thus we live in a world of recycled images. Baudrillard's is a distinctly bleak postmodern vision. See earlier chapters for reference to specific works by Derrida and Baudrillard.

11 Soper, K. (1995) *What is Nature?* Oxford: Blackwell.

of participants' own interpretations. We might take a handshake as an example. We learn little about people by observing the physical behaviour here unless we understand the human body – in this case the hand – as a tool carrying out a social task. It is what the handshake *represents* that is important.[12] Furthermore, the same observed handshake could signify different things in different contexts, subject to various social norms: a welcome, an agreement, a bet. Harré and collaborators have undertaken an important critique of environmental discourse from this perspective, showing how our environmental concerns are encoded in a language saturated with cultural assumptions. The discourse they refer to as 'Greenspeak' draws much of its rhetorical power, for example, from a mixing of palaeontological, cultural and personal time-frames, so that evidence of climate change over aeons can contribute to sense of imminent ecological crisis.[13] Such an insight seems broadly supportive of the 'postfoundationalist' conception of ESD to be elaborated below, though Harré has, in the past, associated himself with a position of pragmatic scientific realism, in contrast to the thoroughgoing relativism we might deduce from Derrida.[14]

However we define ESD, it is a field in which issues of language, human identity, morality, responsibility and action are implicated in natural processes. There are significant differences, however, among the ways in which we can conceive the usefulness of human signifying systems in understanding 'the real world'; the mere fact of implication falls short of suggesting an approach to ESD. To many, ESD is a field which needs to be underpinned by 'hard' (mathematical/ 'natural'/ physical) science: by such knowledge as we have of how increasing carbon dioxide levels might alter climate, for example. Nevertheless, 'scientific realism' describes a set of philosophical positions rather than being a unitary concept; nor, following chaos theory, can we assume that scientists are discovering a universe that is either stable or predictable.[15] The degree to which scientific representation provides transparent access to objective reality as opposed to the degree to which it is culturally determined is a matter of debate among those who nevertheless share the belief that science has progressed in its efforts to approximate reality. Despite the different emphases on the effects of cultural mediation in the pursuit of science, and despite speculations about the

---

12 Harré, R. (1998) *The Singular Self: an introduction to the psychology of personhood*, London: Sage; Harré, R. and Gillett, G. (1994) *The Discursive Mind*, London: Sage.

13 Harré, R., Brockmeier, J. and Muhlhausler, P. (1999) *Greenspeak: a study of environmental discourse*, London: Sage.

14 Bhaskar, R. and Harré, R. (1990) *Harré and his Critics*, Oxford: Blackwell.

15 See, for example, Gonzalez-Gaudiano, E. (2001) Complexity in Environmental Education, *Educational Philosophy and Theory* 33/2, 153–166.

emergence of a 'postmodern' science, however,[16] scientific-realist assumptions about ESD, as defined here, tend to imply a fairly traditional teaching model, valorizing both transmission and rigorous control over processes. According to such a model, student perceptions and 'feelings' about the environment may or may nor be considered valid or helpful. Language and discussion, artistic representation and debate can certainly be useful, but ultimately in the service of clarifying ideas and processes which are essentially the product of the mathematical, 'natural' sciences, or of some new post-Hegelian process-orientated science in which human thoughts and feelings might be seen as part of a pattern of natural emergence (but only if rightly understood in relation to a new 'grand narrative'); if debate serves functions other than this by valorizing all perspectives equally, it can be positively misleading. Remember Plato's cave!

It can be argued that some who claim scientific realism, such as Roy Bhaskar, are better described as critical realists.[17] The critical-realist position as interpreted within ESD (in the spirit of John Fien's words: 'We believe that the environmental crisis is first and foremost a social crisis'[18]) tends to locate 'reality' within the social, or, rather, conflates the social and the environmental, thus seeing ESD as existentially dependent on the human sciences, which is not quite Bhaskar's position. Bhaskar sees the desirability of understanding the articulation between natural and social systems in the move towards social justice. To more naïve critical realists, environmental and ecological issues are simply taken as social issues, and the quests for sustainability and social justice then become not only interdependent but mutually compatible.

Historically, the critical-realist position described here, like Bhaskar's, is essentially Marxist. It takes as a given that capitalism has depleted environmental resources and distributed them inequitably. In the spirit of radical educators such as Paolo Freire, the oppressed must be made to understand the forces that have dominated them in order to undertake their overthrow. Social justice and environmental sustainability are key elements of the better world that can then develop.[19] Such an approach to education certainly invites problematization and critical reflection on action, but only where it promotes certain answers. It retains a belief in false consciousness and posits a model of ESD that is strongly teleological; certain views about

---

[16] Gare, A.E. (1994) *Postmodernism and the Environmental Crisis*, London: Routledge; Littledyke, M. (1997) 'Science Education for Environmental Awareness in a Postmodern World', *Environmental Education Research* 2/2, 197–214.

[17] Bhaskar, R. (1986) *Scientific Realism and Human Emancipation*, Bristol: Verso.

[18] Fien, J. (ed.) (1993) *Environmental Education: a pathway to sustainability*, Victoria, Australia: Deakin University, p. 4.

[19] See Chapter 5, Note 3.

the environment are clearly still aberrant. However, the critical-realist differs from scientific-realist positions in valorizing political over supposedly disinterested scientific action, and in seeing, if only by default, the natural sciences as existentially dependent on the human sciences as well as the other way around.

However, the sustainable development project as a whole might be said to rest on some valorization of the critical-realist position, in that the same set of potential policies aims to bring about economic development, social justice and environmental sustainability, in forms such as biodiversity and pollution control. Similarly, science is still looked to for understanding of, and responses to, environmental problems, even where these are caused by industrial modernization. Thus social reformers, particularly those in the Marxist tradition, often adopt, or attempt to adopt, a stance that is both scientific- and critical-realist in the terms above.

But how valid is such a stance? It is subject to critique on three fronts: it fails to acknowledge the full impact of structuralist and poststructuralist perspectives, even where its adherents pay lipservice to either or both of these movements in cultural theory; it ignores the linguistic turn subsequent to logical positivism, as most clearly evident in Wittgenstein's *Philosophical Investigations*; and it misinterprets the identification of human praxis as a link between biophysical and social reality as a means to understand the former by way of the latter.

Structuralism and poststructuralism are movements in social and cultural studies derived from Saussurean linguistics: specifically the insight that meaning is not derived from natural correspondence (except in cases such as onomatopoeia) but from systems of difference.[20] In other words, since the connection between a signifier and a signified is apparently arbitrary, our understandings are marked out by difference rather than likeness; for instance, we understand 'dog' as 'not cat', 'not fox' and so on, since we cannot identify the word 'dog' as having any truly logical connection to any referent. Structuralists accepted that human meaning is relational and developed new forms of social and cultural inquiry as a result, such as Lévi-Strauss's myth-based anthropology.[21] Structuralism, therefore, can claim validity as a set of approaches to understanding the human, but not the natural, sphere. Nevertheless, structuralist and poststructuralist insights (the latter to a lesser extent) have been heavily influential in the development of socially critical theory, and thus in the critical-realist approaches to ESD that are among its applications.

---

[20] Culler, J. (1976) *Saussure*, London: Fontana. See also references in earlier chapters.

[21] See Chapter 6, Note 11.

Wittgenstein's linguistic turn was also influenced by linguistics: in this case, it seems, more by the speech-act theory of J.L. Austin than directly by Saussure. The influence of Austin's discussions about the performative power of language is clear in Wittgenstein's Blue and Brown Books, and in the *Philosophical Investigations* developed from the thinking contained in them.[22] Wittgenstein's early work, culminating in the *Tractatus*, in which language is seen as conveying logical propositions, is superseded by work in which meaning and truth are contained within language rather than *vice versa*.[23] In terms of the present discussion, Wittgenstein arrived at a similar position to the structuralists in one important sense: language, human reasoning and even human observation – indeed, all rule-governed forms of life – do not give us verifiable access to objective truth. To follow Wittgenstein in this is surely to accept, at the very least, that the language-games we play in pursuit of social progress cannot be understood with reference to biophysical reality.

Yet a number of highly respected late twentieth century figures have argued that there are not only perceivable but potentially verifiable links between human/social and biophysical realities, including Bhaskar, in *Scientific Realism and Human Emancipation* and Jurgen Habermas, particularly in the *Theory of Communicative Action*.[24]

Both Bhaskar and Habermas argue that human praxis provides the link between material reality and social progress, and each argues for social progress based on an exploitation of this realization. Both claim that human/social reality is dependent on biophysical reality; crucially to the argument being developed here, however, neither claims the reverse.

For example, Bhaskar, while acknowledging the interdependence of natural and social systems (with practical activity mediating between them), does not see the social as reducible to the natural. To Bhaskar, the human sciences are 'taxonomically and causally *irreducible* but *dependent* modes of matter'.[25] The human sciences thus have an existential dependence on the

---

[22] The Blue and Brown Books of Wittgenstein are essentially compilations of lecture notes. They provide insights into several elements of Wittgenstein's thinking that appear subsequently in the *Philosophical Investigations*. J.L. Austin is noted for his work on the performative power of language: i.e. the power of language to make things happen in the real world via human action. Austin, J.L. (1965) *How To Do Things With Words*, Oxford: Oxford University Press; Wittgenstein, L. (1964) *Preliminary Studies for the 'Philosophical Investigations'*: *generally known as the Blue and Brown books*, Oxford: Blackwell.

[23] Wittgenstein, L. (1974) *Tractatus Logico-Philosophicus*, London: Routledge.

[24] Habermas, J. (1984) *Theory of Communicative Action* Vol.1: Reason and the Rationalization of Society, Boston: Beacon Press.

[25] Bhaskar, 1986, p. 113.

natural sciences, but not *vice-versa*: 'human phenomena are ... constrained (but not exclusively determined) by natural laws'.[26]

Nevertheless, it is clear that, to Bhaskar, not only human activity, but also our understanding of it, is constrained by biophysical reality. What he does not claim, in contradistinction to Fien and others in ESD, is that nature can in some way be 'read off' from society. While Bhaskar is a Marxist, such a material view of history is not limited to the Marxist tradition. The historian Fernand Braudel, for example, distinguished between the 'event time' of human political concerns and the '*longue durée*' of cultural transformation determined by response to environmental change.[27]

As far as ESD is concerned, Bhaskar, Braudel and others offer the potential of a conceptual framework for understanding social change as dependent on biophysical reality, transformed through human praxis. However, it is important to retain sense of the hierarchy of elements within this relationship. Human praxis can be understood with reference to the material conditions in which it is grounded, but this does not imply the reverse. Ontological realism does not imply full epistemological realism. Bhaskar is not claiming here that social understandings determine biophysical understandings, such that human praxis can substantially transform biophysical reality to meet both social and environmental aims, which is the position at least implied by much of the critical theory within ESD – even though, as the work of Braudel has shown, cultural adaptation to climate and landscape does result in, for example, differential productivity from the land. Climate change can be cited as an example of humanity affecting the rest of nature. However, there is a large credibility gap between the claim that people are, in some measure, contributing to global warming (at least according to the precautionary principle; it is very difficult to weight the factors involved in this[28]) and the claim that we can pursue an agenda that will bring about simultaneous increase in the quality

---

[26] *Ibid.* p. 113.

[27] Braudel, F. (1981) (ed. Reynolds, S.) 'Structures of Everyday Life: the limits of the possible', Part 1 of *Civilisation and Capitalism, 15th–18th Century*, London: Collins.

[28] According to the precautionary principle, action should be taken in response to a perceived threat or danger when there are reasonable grounds to believe that safety might be compromised. If the precautionary principle is not adopted, action should only follow the production of scientific proof. Clearly, as regards the 'big' environmental questions, there has been considerable debate about the need to adhere to the precautionary principle. Climate change is a case in point. If the precautionary principle is adopted, there are grounds for acting against global warming on the assumption that modern human practices contribute to it; however, it is very difficult to provide incontrovertible proof that this is in fact the case.

of human life and environmental sustainability, or even predictable climate change. The second remains Utopian.

Habermas is also often cited by critical theorists within education, and his *Theory of Communicative Action* again attempts to locate social action within the 'real world' (Habermas takes Popper's 'Worlds 1, 2 and 3' as his starting point), but sees communicative action, along with other forms of social action, as indirectly mediated via intentions and interpersonal relationships. Although Habermas does not consider biophysical reality explicitly, it is clear, again, that nature cannot simply be 'read off' from social action. Indeed, while certain forms of action – teleological and strategic – presuppose one unified objective reality, social actions are inevitably also dependent on a pre-existing social and psychological world. Thus, as with Bhaskar, education and other forms of social action cannot be used with any certainty to bring about positive change in the biophysical sphere.

In conclusion, both Bhaskar and Habermas may be ontologically realist (i.e. they believe in the absolute reality of existence), but neither provides support for the kind of critical-realist position adopted in ESD, in which social and environmental aims are conflated, with the latter often seen as a subset of the former rather than the other way round.

The implications of this for ESD – indeed, for the whole political project of sustainable development – are simple but potentially disturbing. There is no valid reason to associate the quest for social justice with that for environmental sustainability. Social aims can be pursued, using our sociocultural ways of knowing, or our influence on the biosphere can be measured, using our scientific understanding of ecology, but there is no reason to suppose the two are compatible; in fact, the reverse might be the case. For example, crushing totalitarianism might be the most effective means of ensuring environmental sustainability. A plethora of new laws might include forbidding tourism and the use of electrical appliances after a certain time in the evening.

Educationally, to acknowledge this fully is to enter a minefield. To indulge in a little poetic licence: if educating for sustainable development is a quest to change 'hearts and minds', it is not helpful to such a quest if hearts and minds pull in opposing directions.

However, the problem is less acute if the pretence is dropped that different ways of knowing are compatible. Accepting that curricular disciplines do not 'add up' as regards their messages for us about environmental action, for example, would allow us to continue an unrestrained debate about environmental issues (however defined). We could then evaluate what we agreed with reference to what seemed to work, by whatever criteria we chose.

Such alternative positions to the scientific and critical realist might be characterized as 'postfoundationalist' and 'relativist'. A postfoundationalist position retains a degree of realism in that there is assumed to be a real world of nature that is under threat. There are held to be a number of valid ways of looking at this threat, however, and at our relationship to nature more generally, and they will, by their differential adoption, have differential consequences on the biosphere, though none can be held validly to underpin the others. C.A Bowers' concern with the 'root metaphors' of Western modernist thinking, alongside his rejection of the critical realism of Freire and others, can be seen as such a position, though it is not a term Bowers himself uses.[29] 'Postfoundationalist' does not necessarily imply 'uncommitted' or even 'undogmatic', but it does accept that there can be other, not easily commensurable, 'truths' about the environment. Educators with this approach will tend to acknowledge the possibility of plural valid responses to environmental issues, and be less teleological than scientific or critical realists, in the sense of looser prescription of the desirable outcomes of ESD. This postfoundationalist position can be contrasted with one of thoroughgoing relativism.

A fully relativist position will acknowledge only perceptions of the environment. The referent is either non-existent or unidentifiable; at most, the unknowable Other. Conceptions of nature are thus mere simulacra; our realities are textual, virtual and socially constructed, and they have no stable meanings. It is to be expected that many of the thinkers we associate with this position (including Derrida and Baudrillard, depending on interpretation) have little interest in what they might dismiss as the Romantic grand narratives of nature and ecology. Few environmentalists adopt a position akin to this. Arguably, an exception is Ingolfur Bluehdorn, whose interest in the Green movement has led him to reject the old polarities on which it was based (such as nature-society) and to write about a post-ecological politics which celebrates private-ironist and other deconstructive tendencies within environmental thought rather than a commitment to sustainability.[30] Such a view might support ESD as 'education around the environment' (to quote John Foster[31]) but would be likely heartily to reject its usual teleology.

None of these positions, or those, which might comprise any more elaborate or convincing taxonomy, can claim absolute legitimization. The degree to which any might make such a claim is dependent to a large degree

---

29 Bowers, C.A. (2002) 'Towards an Eco-Justice Pedagogy', *Environmental Education Research*, special edition 'On the Possibility of Education for Sustainable Development' 8/1, 21–34.

30 Bluehdorn, I. (2000) *Post-Ecological Politics: social theory and the abdication of the ecologist paradigm* (London/New York: Routledge).

31 Unpublished remark made at a Centre for Research in Education and the Environment (CREE) seminar, University of Bath, 1999.

on the position one takes concerning the relationship of human sign systems (language and other cultural and social practice) in relation to external reality; the relationship of signifier not just to signified, but to referent. Scientific-realist positions, after Plato, though acknowledging cultural influences to differing extents, will tend to see language as somehow conveying reality: as a mirror or vehicle. In this case, language and personal meaning can be used as means to understanding (e.g. via dialectic or instruction), but can also seriously mislead (e.g. via political rhetoric or artistic style). Post-Saussurean positions on language render such assumptions about language highly questionable. The logic of a system of human meanings is, according to post-Saussurean structuralism, internally relational and not externally verifiable; according to post-structuralists, there is no logic to it at all. The critical-realist position is also rendered problematic by an understanding of language derived from Saussure and his successors, given that it seems to accept (indeed, depend on) structural social and cultural analysis while assuming that understanding of the biophysical environment can be conflated with the understanding of the social and the cultural: the very antithesis of the premise of structuralism. Both postfoundationalist and relativist approaches will accept, or move beyond (in the case of poststructuralism and thorough-going relativism), the structuralists' distinction between the internal relational logic of systems of signs and the assumption of any obvious connection to an objective referent, logical or otherwise. The biosphere simply cannot be 'known'. Relativist positions hold that human beings are trapped in a world of signs that is at best self-referential and at worst inherently unstable or simply incomprehensible. The latter positions pose even greater problems for environmental educators, yet can be justified.

The position taken in this present publication is inherently postfoundationalist in calling for acceptance of differing positions but retaining a belief in the potential of ESD to help bring about some sort of sustainability. Indeed, none of the above positions is necessarily hopeless in this respect. Even a relativist (after Rorty or Derrida, perhaps) can call for deference to an Other. If we cannot know Nature, at least we can defer to its Otherness; perhaps the policy option of leaving well alone is one that has been too little adopted. Neither does the adoption of a postfoundational position infer that there can be no common ground between environmental educators, nor that one set of assumptions and procedures might not prove more effective than another in a given context. The *sensus communis* which Gadamer, for example, sees as an important indicator of our historically effected consciousness,[32] and for which Kant, too, had considerable respect, tells us that there cannot be many with an interest in environment generally

---

[32] Gadamer, H-G. (1975) *Truth and Method*, London: Sheed and Ward.

who do not share some apparently common concern for a better, cleaner, healthier, or, at least, not-worse biophysical environment. There are not likely to be many people who would not subscribe to such sentiments, though critical realists might see the issues as subsumed within a programme for social, rather than merely environmental, change. At this level of generality (only), there can be some agreement about the aims or, at least, some of the objectives of ESD; at this level, ESD certainly allows for pluralism. This field, like all others, is subject to interpretation.

The recent ESD discourse in the UK and several other countries recently has put increased emphasis on 'Sustainable Development Education' rather than 'Environmental Education'.[33] It may be the hope of some that this reorientation will give increased clarity of focus and aims. However, it is already acknowledged in the curriculum development literature that 'sustainable development' is not an unproblematic term, despite its origins in Gro Haarlem Brundtland's ideal of meeting the needs of the present while not compromising the ability of future generations to meet their own needs. The term is effectively redefined in the latest curriculum guidance provided for teachers in England and Wales, for example, with seven key concepts held to be central to it (interdependence; citizenship and stewardship; needs and rights of future generations; diversity; quality of life, equity and justice; sustainable change, and uncertainty and precaution).[34] If the term were unidimensional and unproblematic across all the language games in which it appears, there would be validity in such a breakdown of its elements. In reality, increased reflection on the term and its uses is unlikely to result in greater consensus, unless there is universal aspiration towards a consensual definition. ESD is particularly problematic in this regard because 'sustainable development' is a good example of a 'paradoxical compound policy slogan', the appeal of which is that it can allow those of widely differing views to 'buy into' it to some extent.[35] In the words of Norman Fairclough, it has high 'ambivalence potential'.[36] In this case, on the most obvious level, economic interests are served by 'development' while ecological concerns are addressed by 'sustainable'; at the same time, economic interests are served by 'sustaining' profits, investments etc.; the compound term, however, allows us to feel that the two key terms are unproblematically complementary: that we can 'have our cake and eat it',

---

[33] See beginning of Chapter 7.

[34] In 2002, guidance for teaching sustainable development issues appeared on the National Curriculum website at www.nc.uk.net/esd.

[35] Stables, A. (1996) Paradox in Compound Educational Policy Slogans, *British Journal of Educational Studies*, 44/2, 159–167.

[36] Fairclough, N. (1995) *Critical Discourse Analysis*, London: Longman, pp.112–119, 173–174.

thus widely conflicting interests are combined into what is intended to serve as a single regulative ideal. Practically, such slogans can have wide popular appeal, though it is perhaps too early to claim this for 'sustainable development'. However, it is important to bear in mind that the implementations and practical outcomes of such policies are highly unpredictable. The variety in the existing realization of ESD within school curricula might be seen as compelling evidence of this. Policies work for democratic politicians to some extent merely by allowing those politicians to be re-elected, but the popular appeal of a policy does not predetermine even the nature, let alone the effectiveness, of its outcomes when these are evaluated in any more than crudely populist terms. Sustainable development education may, therefore, prove an even more contested field than Environmental Education, both because it is a more sophisticated, and thus potentially ambiguous, compound term, and because it currently enjoys even less popular appeal in schools and colleges. Some environmental educators have indeed expressed severe doubts about its adoption.[37]

How should educators, who tend to share the general aspiration towards a better, cleaner, less depleted world but who approach ESD from widely differing perspectives and with differing preconceptions, work with their students within this contested field? To what extent might the *sensus communis* allow us to make some general statements in relation to teaching processes? (By 'teaching processes' I mean those generic processes to do with teaching and learning, in whatever field.) In this area we can suppose a degree of loose consensus concerning three areas, without assuming any consensus regarding their appropriate balance: the importance of knowledge (practical and theoretical), the importance of cultural sensitivity (involving some degree of empathy), and the importance of enterprise, or empowerment. In ESD, it is useful to think of such broad educational objectives in relation to the development of functional, cultural and critical environmental literacies, thus making possible the relating of pedagogical processes in ESD to those in other areas.

An introduction to these forms of environmental literacy has been provided in Chapters 6 and 7. It is important to note here that, as a focus of differing disciplinary traditions, the environment can be understood in various ways, so even agreement on what should constitute functional environmental literacy cannot be taken for granted. Nevertheless, given the

---

[37] E.g. Bob Jickling (1992) 'Why I Don't Want My Children To Be Educated For Sustainable Development', *Journal of Environmental Education* 33/4, 5–8.

dominance of instrumental rationality in modern cultural practice,[38] and thus in the pursuit of modern science, the teaching and learning of the basics of scientific ecology is an example of one area that is bound to underpin the development of such a 'literacy', especially in advanced technological societies.

However, functionality without cultural sensitivity and critical reflection is potentially as destructive as constructive, even if it is a functionality that takes some account of, say, resource management and social and environmental consequence. Knowing about ecology does not ensure ecologically responsible behaviour, where such knowledge forms part of a tradition that eschews considerations of value, or values only 'progress' as measured in narrowly anthropocentric terms. Certainly, in terms of purely instrumental rationality, and arguably even with respect to social justice, a 'sustainable' ecosystem does not guarantee a world worth living in; a dictatorship could be more ecologically responsible than a democracy, for example. Even 'sustainable development' might be unbearable, if it simply meant the union of economic growth and environmental sustainability – even if it included more equitable distribution of resources – because it might be achieved without any consideration of other important value domains, such as the aesthetic.

For the world to be worth living in, we surely need high levels of both cultural and critical environmental literacies, in order that we can acknowledge that we live in an ecosystem the future of which is dependent on our moral choices, feel empowered to act for the environment in ways that seem apposite, and become better able to evaluate the effects of our, and others', actions with respect to the environment.

What should the role of the teacher be in such a contested field? In terms of the typology above, it cannot simply be to develop functional environmental literacy, important though this is. Such a simple outcome orientation is untenable when we cannot assume agreement over either ends or means. In effect, the need to develop cultural and critical environmental literacies demands a critical retrospective on the histories that have brought us to an appreciation of ecological crisis: the history of science, for example, and of the increasingly secular humanism that has driven and interpreted it. In conclusion, ESD therefore calls for a critical retrospective on humanist modernity, inspired by a sense that the cultural practices through which we

---

38 By 'instrumental rationality' I refer to Habermas (1972: *Knowledge and Human Interest*, Boston: Beacon) and the idea of applied scientific knowledge used to gain control over nature for technological ends. Such knowledge is highly valued in modern societies, hence the high curricular status of science and technology *vis-à-vis* the arts and social sciences (though there is also a Platonic legacy here, as was argued in Chapter 6).

have been nurtured may be, unless modified, inadequate bases for the future, however much we are indebted and attached to them.

In terms of teaching, this implies a reconceptualization of environment from principally cross-disciplinary to within-disciplinary concern, with inter-disciplinarity acknowledged as driven by a dialogue between specialism and shared concern in which 'ways of knowing' are seen as affecting the known as well as the process by which it is known. The search then becomes less for an holistic approach to ESD and more for the best way to develop, and thus modify, the disciplines in a period of ecological crisis. If we are to take the later Wittgenstein (and others) seriously, environment should be seen as a topic within fields rather than across fields because fields, not topics, define and limit meanings. Nevertheless, in each discipline there remains scope for an increased focus on how human and non-human activity are mutually implicated.

Take, for example, the study of literature. A body of ecocritical work has arisen in recent years, some of it looking explicitly at literary approaches to the human-nature relationship, such as Lawrence Buell's criteria for environmental writing.[39] There remains much scope for new and accessible readings of canonical works stemming from our ecological concerns. A recent European Union-funded project, based in the Universities of Bath, Ghent and Oporto, attempted to develop this and other ideas for creative classroom use.[40] This project developed five foci based on the various possible relationships between 'environment' and 'text' in literary and media studies, from ecocritical readings of literary texts (Focus 1) to the creation of texts exploring environmental issues (Focus 3) and consideration of the environment itself as text (Focus 4). Thus the aim was to explore the human-nature relationship through good literature and media education rather than distorting the curriculum by studying certain texts merely as the embodiment of environmental and ecological themes and issues. There must be scope for other subjects to give more attention to environmental issues without the crude imposition of 'sustainable development' as a cross-curricular theme or aim assuming validity free of context. For example, the work of Fernand Braudel and, more recently, of Simon Schama show clearly how cultural and social histories can be studied within broader environmental contexts.

---

[39] Buell, L. (1995) *The Environmental Imagination: Thoreau, nature writing and the formation of American culture*, Cambridge, MA: Harvard University Press, p. 7.

[40] Bishop, K., Reid, A., Stables, A., Lencastre, M., Stoer, S. and Soetaert, R. (2000) 'Developing Environmental Awareness Through Literature and Media Education: curriculum development in the context of teachers' practice', *Canadian Journal of Environmental Education* 5, 268–286.

Our late-modern, or post-modern, consciousnesses are formed by the ways of thinking that have brought us to the realization of environmental crisis. Herein lie both the threat of a double-bind and our hope for the future. We are continuously able to reflect on and modify such mental structures, as Kant suggested (whether or not such reflection is driven purely by experience). Given the impossibility of constraining ESD within a narrowly defined set of aims and measurable outcomes, we should rather take the ever-present opportunity of examining the cultural, social and academic practices of our recent histories from the viewpoint of our environmentally-concerned present. Alongside developing functional environmental literacy, in part through a basic grounding in scientific ecology, education could be more strongly orientated to developing increased meta-awareness of dominant cultural practices within our own societies, and of the cultural practices of others. Above all, as educators, we are aiming to empower those who will live in the world of the future to draw their own conclusions in circumstances that are bound to be different from our own. They should then be better able, individually and co-operatively, to act in ways that seem to them appropriate to purpose.

The emphasis on individual empowerment and responsibility as educational aims is maintained in the next chapter, in which approaches to classroom practice are discussed with reference to their capacity to promote positive personal and social identities.

Chapter 9

Why Teach? Effective Teaching as Positive Identity Development

Education may have uncertain outcomes, and may not be able to deliver social objectives in clearly identifiable ways, but this is not to say that the minutiae of classroom practice cannot usefully be seen as bearing on other important issues. Here, the role of classroom interactions, of various sorts, is considered in relation to its possible effects on the development of the learner's broader identity, as identity development serves as a possible aim of a less teleological educational programme.[1]

Previous research has shown strong links between learner self-image and orientation to schooling. However, in most of the current literature, effective teaching is considered largely in terms of short term output measures, and the theoretical link between effective teaching and the development of a positive self-identity is not developed in empirical studies of classrooms. However, in a context of individualized risk taking, uncertain outcomes and the lack of unquestioned social objectives for education, the development of personal qualities such as confidence and adaptability can be seen as an increasingly important educational aim. This chapter attempts to give a working definition of positive identity development, uses the work of Rom Harré and others to show how teaching methods could be reorientated towards developing more positive self-identities,[2] and explores possibilities for more focused, empirical work in this area.

[1] Permission has been granted by Taylor and Francis to reproduce material in this chapter from Stables, A., Jones, S. and Morgan, C. (1999) 'Educating for Significant Events: the application of Harre's social reality matrix across the lower secondary school curriculum', *Journal of Curriculum Studies* 31/4, 449–461. See also <http://www.tandf.co.uk>. Acknowledgement is also due to Sonia Jones and Carol Morgan for their contributions to the *JCS* article, particularly for the exemplar sections relating to, respectively, mathematics and modern foreign languages teaching.
[2] See Harré, R. (1983) *Personal Being: a theory for individual psychology*, Oxford: Blackwell.

One of the key themes to emerge from Joan Rudduck *et al*'s study of students' views on secondary schooling[3] is that learner self-image plays a crucial role in determining orientation to school work. Indeed, by the middle years of secondary education, self-image as academic failure or success to a large extent seems to drive the whole experience of school. As part of this study, Chaplain shows disengaged students as scoring low on a 'self-concept as a learner scale' and goes on to summarise how their disengagement adversely colours all aspects of their school lives.

Given the well established link between motivation and learning, this is hardly surprising. Ironically, however, the current interest in effective teaching and learning among educational researchers and policy makers tends to evaluate effective teaching solely in terms of measurable results and fails to find any obvious links between indicators of motivation and achievement. This certainly poses problems for the development of a pragmatic, learner-centred view of education, in which self-validation of processes must play a key role.

The failure of research to link measures of motivation to levels of success, while the theoretical and psychological literature remains firm in its commitment to such a link, may have a number of possible explanations.[4] It may be that researchers are using too narrow a view of indicators of motivation, taking pupil interest in lessons to be interest in subjects, for example, when, in fact, students are attracted merely by certain kinds of activity and of teaching. It may be that curriculum subjects change so radically from phase to phase or year to year that neither motivation nor achievement is stable over time, so the links between the two are obscured; there is certainly evidence in the research literature of 'curricular discontinuity' between educational phases, such as the 'jump' from GCSE to A Level in England in the 1990s.[5] It may be that the kind of learning required to gain improved standardized test scores is not 'deep' enough to touch on issues of self-identity. What remains clear is that the role of pedagogical practice in developing, or challenging, self-identity is being little explored, while the psychological literature, as well as studies such as

---

[3] Rudduck, J., Chaplain, R. and Wallace, G. (eds) (1996) *School Improvement: what can pupils tell us?* London: David Fulton.

[4] See also Chapter 3.

[5] See, for example, Stables, A. and Stables, S. (1995) 'Gender Differences in Students' Approaches to A Level Subject Choices and Perceptions of A Level Subjects: a study of first-year A level students in a tertiary college', *Educational Research* 37/1, 39–51, and (1996) Modern Languages at A-Level: the danger of curricular discontinuity, *Language Learning Journal* 14, 50–52. One of the issues discussed here is the 'jump' in level from GCSE to Advanced Level work in England, particularly in certain subjects, including modern foreign languages.

Rudduck, Chaplain and Wallace's, stresses the centrality of positive self-identity for, in or through significant learning.

At a theoretical level, Rom Harré's work on the Identity Project has proved useful in generating models for classroom practice with relation to identity change. Such work has been able to show the potential for much more focused attention to be given to identity development in the planning and execution of classroom activities.

In the early 1990s, Malcolm Ross and his collaborators at Exeter University constructed and tested a model for assessing creative arts activity in schools based on the Identity Project.[6] According to this model, Harré's 'social reality matrix', individual identity is dependent on social context, and the work of 'transformation' and 'publication' serves to confirm the individual as moral agent within a moral and social order, resulting both in stronger social identities for the marginalized and in greater self-expression for the socially established. Thus the creative process is key both to personal growth and to social order and progress. Socioconstructivist and experiential theories of learning similarly stress that all learning is brought about through the involvement of personal and social activity in a process of personal growth. Thus there would seem to be a case, therefore, for applying Harré's insights to curriculum planning beyond the creative arts, in order to increase student satisfaction from a range of discourses.

Constructivist learning theories hold in common the belief that meaning is generated by individuals by means of new experience modifying existing patterns of thought and response which have been formed by cumulative response to previous experience.[7] Socioconstructivist approaches, after Vygotsky[8] and Berger and Luckmann,[9] lay particular stress on the personal reformulation of understanding in language as a result of interpersonal activity. A broader tradition of learning through doing, after Dewey, and particularly his concept of 'instrumentalism', stresses in more general terms the need for learners to be engaged actively in meaningful personal experience, i.e. that learning, in any domain, needs to appear relevant to the learner and must engage him/her in undertaking real tasks involving the

6   Ross, M., Radnor, H., Mitchell, S. and Brierton, C. (1993) *Assessing Achievement in the Arts*, Buckingham: Open University Press.
7   E.g. Glaserfeld, E. von (1995) *Radical Constructivism: a way of knowing and learning*, London: Falmer.
8   Vygotsky, L.S. (1962) *Thought and Language*, Cambridge, Mass.: MIT and (1978) *Mind in Society: the development of higher psychological processes*, Cambridge, Mass.: Harvard University Press.
9   Berger, P. and Luckmann, T. (1966) *The Social Construction of Reality: a treatise on the construction of knowledge*, New York: Doubleday.

exercise of personal initiative, within the context of the living culture that exists beyond as well as within the school.[10]

Constructivism suggests that the effectiveness of the learning experience is dependent on its perceived relevance by the learner; theories of active learning (after Dewey) stress that the learner should be engaged in purposive and enjoyable activity and not merely recognising something as true. Even the vocational curriculum in England and Wales has been criticised for tending not to adhere sufficiently to this principle.[11] Research by writers committed to active and experiential learning has tended to show that much classroom time is devoted to the development of merely procedural, rather than principled, knowledge.[12] Indeed, the uneven power relationship between teacher and taught makes a genuine dialogue of inquiry difficult in schools.[13] Much of what goes on in schools appears to be about coping with institutional demands, or learning to avoid them as much as possible, rather than learning associated with personal transformation. Furthermore, many interpretations of socioconstructivism in the classroom ignore issues of disciplinarity; there is little emphasis in the literature on small group work, for example, on the collective and individual mastery of subject-specific discourses, even though, in a general way, there is both an increasing acknowledgment of the importance of 'genre' and a tendency to claim that collaborative work can aid 'scientific thinking' and the like.[14]

The joint emphases on relevance and activity as the preconditions for effective learning presuppose a cycle of engagement, preparation and completion in the teaching-learning situation as experienced by the learner. An alternative exposition is that all meaningful learning must involve the kind of production over which the learner feels a sense of responsibility, relevance and empowerment. In other words, the learning cycle must encompass some kind of significant event: something akin to the humanist

---

[10] Dewey, J. (1910) *Educational Essays*, London: Blackie and (1916) 'Vocational Aspects of Education', in *Democracy and Education*, New York: The Free Press, 306–320.

[11] Hyland, T. (1993) 'Vocational Reconstruction and Dewey's Instrumentalism', *Oxford Review of Education* 19/1, 89–100.

[12] Edwards, D. and Mercer, N. (1987) *Common Knowledge: the development of understanding in the classroom*, London: Routledge.

[13] Young, R. (1992) *Critical Theory and Classroom Talk*, Clevedon: Multilingual Matters.

[14] E.g. much of the work in Kate Norman (ed.) (1992) *Thinking Voices: the work of the National Oracy Project*, London: Hodder and Stoughton. Much of the material for this volume is drawn from local 'oracy projects' carried out in British schools in the 1980s. Also, Mercer, N. (2000) *Words and Minds*, London: Routledge. In fact, these points hold true for a large amount of literature in this area, some of which is referred to in Mercer.

psychologist Maslow's 'peak experience', a moment of self-actualization, signifying completion, in terms of production, performance or achieved insight.[15] The formal curriculum is rarely, if ever, framed in these terms, however, but is rather atomistic, with related elements linked thematically but not in terms of building towards significance. It is down to the individual teacher, for example, to turn the National Curriculum in England and Wales in any given subject into a dynamic series of learning experiences with a sense of cumulative purpose.

In *Personal Being*, Harré conceptualises personal and social action along three dimensions, which he terms Agency, Display and Realization. Each dimension has two axes: Agency can be active or passive; Display can be private or public; Realization can be individual or collective. Personal development consists of a series of Identity Projects, each of which follows the same sequence, from Conventionalization through Appropriation to Transformation to Publication.

Ross *et al* define each of the three key terms here with relation to arts education. Conventionalization refers to personal attunement to cultural norms, through which self expression must occur, so that 'the child's products and responses are offered as additions to the conventional wisdom of society, and she herself becomes a bearer of the culture'.[16] Thus Conventionalization is both the beginning and the end of the cycle.

Appropriation is the process of taking on board for oneself the conventions of the culture for the expression of personal feeling. A belief in Harré's notion of appropriation implies a duty on the part of schools to teach children about the means by which feeling can legitimately be expressed within society, according to Ross. Harré himself emphasizes the importance of 'institutions of self-knowledge', whereby what Western culture often takes to be 'an individual's own isolated mental activity' is, in fact, 'a social process involving others in quite definite social relations to the person at the centre of the cognitive work'. Personal identity projects therefore demand an understanding of 'maxims and rules...subject to public assessment as to their compatibility with local moral orders': Harré cites 'the furore created by the publication of a guide to successful suicide published by the EXIT society'.[17] Thus curriculum models arising from Harré must operate within considerably more controlled frameworks than that provided by a simple desire to allow students engaged self-expression. This semi-Foucauldian acknowledgment of the power of situated discourses, coupled with a more

---

[15] Maslow, A.H. and Chiang, H-M. (1977) *The Healthy Personality*, London: D. Van Nostrand; Maslow, A.H. (1968) *Towards a Psychology of Being*, New York: Litton.

[16] Ross *et al.* p. 53.

[17] Quotations from Harré (1983), ps. 259, 262. The EXIT Society campaign for voluntary euthanasia.

general view of the child as evolving social and civic agent, helps to increase the appeal of Harré's model to those interested in teaching and learning in schools and colleges, as students have to develop their identities while negotiating complex disciplinary structures.[18] At the risk of over-simplification, Harré's model has some potential to coalesce what are often seen as the 'social' and 'educational' functions of schooling, not least in the middle and lower secondary years.

Transformation, with respect to the arts, refers to the learner's 'aesthetic project', by means of which feeling is represented in new forms of particular significance to their creator. Ross and collaborators' clear message for arts educators is that Appropriation and Transformation are essentially acts over which the child must retain ownership, but that good teaching involves the teacher's ability to 'identify (and identify with)' what the child is doing, as well as the teacher having a responsibility to ensure the student has the social and moral understanding implicit in successful appropriation (see above).[19]

Transformation leads to publication, at which point 'an actor stands on the threshold of radical recategorization', as social response to the publication could, *in extremis*, label him/her as anything from a madman to a genius. Following publication, 'the personal innovation is taken up into the conventions of the social order in which it has been publicized' i.e. there is a new form of conventionalization, and the cycle can begin afresh.[20]

Harré's model is clearly applicable to activity in the creative arts, as Ross *et al* have shown. However, the application may not seem so obvious in other areas of the curriculum, even though it has an obvious appeal in terms of experiential and socioconstructivist learning theories. There follow, therefore, a series of attempts to apply Harre's cycle to other curriculum areas at secondary level: English, modern foreign languages and mathe-matics. The intended result of such an application is the creation of a model of learning that involves repeated cycles of conventionalization, appro-priation and publication, and which can subsume other curricular elements within a cycle of activity over which the student feels a real sense of ownership. Such a model can be both child- and subject-centred.

---

[18] See Danaher, G., Schirato, T. and Webb, J. (2000) *Understanding Foucault*, London: Sage. Much of Foucault's work concerns the workings of power and subjectivity (in the sense both of personal agency and subjection to power). Power is often conceptualised as working through discursive practices, within which the individual is positioned as both, or either, agent or victim.

[19] Ross *et al* (1993). Quotations from ps. 54, 55.

[20] Quotations from Harré (1983) p. 257.

English

Of the three subjects discussed, English will generally be considered to have the strongest 'creative arts' element. However, its place at the core of the curriculum throughout the English-speaking world means that English must play a number of roles within the curriculum, and this both challenges and, in some respects, gives great freedom to the English teacher. The Cox Report, which laid down the blueprint for English in the National Curriculum in England and Wales, identified five models of English teaching, each of which is reflected (to varying degrees) within the prescribed curriculum: Adult Needs, Personal Growth, Cultural Heritage, Cultural Analysis and Cross-Curricular.[21] Although many aspects of National Curriculum implementation in England and Wales have been critiqued, there is little in the literature to suggest that classroom teachers are not happy with this general classification of the most commonly adopted approaches (though this does not imply, of course, that each model enjoys equal professional support). For the sake of clarity, therefore, in the passage below, Cox's models will be accepted as a fair representation of the range of approaches used in the English classroom.

An expressivist, 'Personal Growth' model of English teaching, characterised by a child-centred approach to literature and many opportunities for relatively unregulated creative writing, can clearly be informed by Harré's model, which can be seen as laying emphasis on the need for conscious planning with relation to appropriation, as well as with regard to transformation and publication. To the tenets of such an approach to English teaching, Harré might stress:

(i) an attention to genre:[22] in other words, both at the appropriation and transformation stages, an awareness of forms and their appropriate uses in context; an awareness that writing (for example) always exists in terms of its form, function, purpose and audience;

(ii) an attention to the power of publication. Much English teaching of recent years has focused on the importance of process vis-à-vis product in English teaching,[23] but Harré stresses the socially, as well as the personally, transformative power of the published work;

[21] DES (Department for Education and Science, UK) (1989) *English for Ages 5 to 16*, London: HMSO. The sources of the five 'Cox models' are not made clear, but they have been used frequently since in teacher education and research.

[22] Kress, G. and Knapp, P. (1992) 'Genre in a Social Theory of Language', *English in Education* 26/2, 4–15.

[23] E.g. D'Arcy, P. (1989) *Making Sense, Shaping Meaning: writing in the context of a capacity-based approach to learning*, Portsmouth, NH: Boynton-Cook.

(iii) with respect to conventionalisation, the power of published work to move, alter perceptions, change minds and even alter genres and the expectations one holds of them.

With respect to the Personal Growth model of English, attention to Harré has the apparent potential to enrich the cycles of creative activity which already occur. Let us now consider how Harré's model might inform a sequence of lessons incorporating strong elements of Cox's four remaining models. In this hypothetical sequence, a piece of classic literature (Cultural Heritage) is discussed by students who are then asked to produce a newspaper front page, using computers, giving news of the key events in the novel or play which have been read and discussed. To be carried out successfully, this activity demands an awareness of journalistic writing and newspaper design (Cultural Analysis), and use of skills (of writing, word-processing and desktop publishing) which are relevant both to the adult world of work (Adult Needs) and to the students' learning in other subjects (Cross-Curricular).

At the Appropriation stage, the students need to 'take on board' the extract from the classic literature. This requires, as well as emotional involvement issuing from attention to a lively reading, awareness of the author's use of generic features for effect (both now and at the time of original publication) and background cultural and contextual knowledge relating to the piece which a modern reader may lack, as well as the ability to make literal sense of the vocabulary and syntactic features of the original writing.

The act of transformation into the students' newspaper stories requires a sophisticated sensitivity to types and purposes of journalistic writing, as well as the adoption of a suitable tone and register for the task at hand with respect to the expectations of the teacher (as the piece's real audience). The act of transformation also requires certain technical skills: of writing, but in this case, also of computing.

The act of publication has often been downplayed in English, despite its 'creative arts' element. Since the Cox Report, in the various iterations of the National Curriculum,[24] there has been greater emphasis in England and Wales on writing for real audiences (i.e. other than the teacher). Harré stresses both the personal risk taken by the creator submitting work for publication, and the significant personal and social change that can arise as a result of publication. Within the discourse community of the English classroom, students' published work should be given pride of place, and greater attention should be given to the effects of individuals' writing on other individuals, the group and the writer him or herself. If this can be

---

[24] E.g. Department for Education (DfE) (1995) *English in the National Curriculum*, London: HMSO.

achieved, student writers will become increasingly sensitive to the power of their work to transform themselves and others and will thus, in turn, become more sensitive both to the literature and media products they encounter, and to the expectations of those they write for: whether teachers in other subjects, themselves (in their notes, for example), employers, potentially significant others whose potential help they seek, or the audiences for their more creative, artistic output.

As the subject among our chosen three with the greatest claim to creative arts status, enrichment of teaching and learning from conscious attention to Harré's model would seem feasible and relatively easy to achieve.

Modern Foreign Languages

When we consider the learning of second and other languages, however, the model requires more sophisticated application, largely because the cultural context for the target language is often relatively alien to the learner.

On one level, modern foreign languages is a curriculum area that could accommodate many of the key features for personal growth noted by Harré relatively unproblematically. If we take Harré's appropriation-transformation-publication cycle, the model of communicative teaching methodology that currently underpins the National Curriculum would seem to align closely with the conditions required at each of these stages.

Appropriation, 'which encompasses processes of development which create minds that are reflections of linguistic forms and social practices'[25] can be promoted via the National Curriculum requirements to 'use language for real purposes ...and learn the use of social conventions';[26] the inclusion of 'cultural awareness' as part of the language programme is also an indication of a view of FL learning understandable in terms of Harré's model.

Transformation processes are indicated in further National Curriculum requirements to 'understand and apply patterns rules and exceptions in language forms and structure [and to] use ... knowledge to experiment with language'.[27] There has been an increasing interest in the raising of awareness of pupils' own language learning strategies and this now features

---

[25] Harré (1983) p. 256.

[26] DfE (Department for Education, UK) (1996) *Foreign Languages in the National Curriculum: modern*, London: HMSO, pp. 2–3.

[27] DfE (1995) *Modern Foreign Languages in the National Curriculum*, London: HMSO, p. 3.

in textbooks as well as in critical literature.[28] Language awareness programmes popular in the 1970s and 80s have also regained popularity, particularly in other European countries.[29] In programmes in the UK this meant that teachers undertook particular language-intensive initiatives (either special days where only the foreign language was spoken or intensive foreign language revision days) in order to heighten pupils' awareness of the special nature of the foreign language. In other countries there is some interest in language awareness activities at primary level where pupils have the opportunity to explore what foreign languages in general might look like (their structure, vocabulary etc).[30] Here there is a link with the notion of transformation in that pupils are alerted to the special properties of language(s). The National Curriculum, in its original iteration, suggested a further possible area of personal empowerment in that 'The World of Imagination and Creativity' was to be included as a separate topic or area of study (Area G in the 'Areas of Experience').[31] Later versions of the National Curriculum were content to suggest imaginative activities as a general recommendation in the general rubrics for their 'Programmes of Study'.[32]

Publication is encouraged by the communicative syllabus with its emphasis on oral performance (taking publication in its widest sense of 'making public'), and the specific cultural constraints of a controlled framework of publication are clear in National Curriculum requirements: 'to vary language to suit context, evidence and purpose'.[33]

However, other factors, relating to classroom practice rather than policy prescriptions, militate against a realization of Harré's model. In a modern foreign language context there is a four-layered identity matrix at work which overlays the interaction already described. In addition to the pupil's own linguistic and social identity formed on a personal and peer level on the one hand and the 'school identity' for the pupil created by the teacher, on the other, there is the double-sided linguistic and cultural identity associated with the

---

[28] Ellis, G. and Sinclair, B. (1989) *Learning to Learn English: a course in learner training*, Cambridge: Cambridge University Press; Grenfell, M. and Harris, V. (1993) How Do Pupils Learn? (Part 1), *Language Learning Journal* 8, 22–25; and Part 2, *LLJ* 9, 7–11; Morgan, C. (1995) 'Cultural Awareness and the National Curriculum', *Language Learning Journal* 12, 9–12.

[29] Hawkins, E. and Perren, G.E. (eds) *Intensive Language Teaching in Schools*, London: Centre for Information on Language Teaching and Research (CILT); Hawkins, E. (ed.) (1988) *Intensive Language Teaching and Learning: initiatives at school level*, London: CILT.

[30] Morgan, C. (unpublished) *The Process of Transfer from the Bilingual Primary School*, University of Bath, Department of Education.

[31] DES (1990) *Modern Foreign Languages for Ages 11 to 16*, London: HMSO.

[32] E.g. DfE (1995) (see Note 26).

[33] DfE (1996) p. 3.

foreign language: there is the school version of, for example, what 'French' is, and what 'being French' is and there is also a native speaker version of this. When it comes to appropriation the pupil is likely to be absorbing a tailored version of linguistic forms and social practices, which may bear little relation to those forms, and practices in action in the target country.

Harré suggests that we may 'gain epistemic access' to ourselves in the process of transformation by using metaphorical discourse (determined by our local context).[34] Unlike the discourse fields available in other subject domains, the linguistic forms available in a modern foreign languages lesson are likely to be extremely impoverished. An emphasis on almost total target language use[35] limits the range of linguistic resources available and the legacy of language used only for functional purposes (despite the nominal inclusion of creative activities) encourages the appropriation of artificially constructed discourse with little opportunity for personal ownership.[36]

In terms of public performance of language, most interaction will be in the classroom where the conditions of production relate to approval by peers and a school version of linguistic and cultural appropriacy. There has been, up to now, little opportunity to interact with target language and culture in action in a real context, although the presence of foreign language assistants and of native speaker teachers, and the inclusion of visits to, and exchanges with, the target country clearly help.

If teachers believe that, to achieve a sense of significance, we need a dynamic series of learning experiences, there is certainly provision for this in terms of linguistic progression in foreign language classrooms.[37] What is missing is any similar building up of a progression in understanding the culture of a foreign country. Cultural awareness, where it appears, deals with information and understanding in a random manner with little sense of gaining a deeper understanding of ourselves (or of others).

If Harré's cycle is to be applied meaningfully to the modern foreign language context, it requires double revolutions: firstly with the pupils' own language and culture and secondly with the target language and culture. In other words there needs to be authenticity of interaction which more closely resembles the interaction of daily life.

---

[34] Harré (1983) p. 283.

[35] DfE (1996) p. 2.

[36] Morgan, C. (1996) 'Creative Writing in Foreign Language Teaching', in Thompson, L. and Millward, P. (eds) *The Teaching of Poetry: European perspectives*, London: Cassell, 44–54.

[37] Byram, M. and Morgan, C. (1994) *Teaching-and-Learning Language-and-Culture*, Clevedon: Multilingual Matters.

One project in 1997 that sought to do this was loosely based on Jones' Shoebox project of 1995.[38] In the later project, pupils considered an aspect of their own culture (in this case 'law and order'), produced relevant materials in their own language and sent it to a classroom in the target country. They then received a similar package from their partner class and were able to contrast and compare the two approaches. A further stage envisaged in a subsequent project was for pupils to communicate electronically (via fax, email or the Internet) to comment on each other's work.

This activity offers the opportunity to appropriate two sets of authentic linguistic forms and social practices, to transform them in a climate of reflexivity and enquiry and to make their products public with due regard to linguistic appropriacy and discussion of cultural appropriacy in terms of pupils' own culture and the target culture. It can be said to mirror the interactive 'socialism' which Harré foregrounds, in that pupils in the foreign receiving classroom will also be taking notice of the English 'products'. With continued contact between the classrooms (or with other classrooms), repeated cycles of conventionalization, appropriation and publication should be possible.

Only when the full implications of language learning as cultural learning have been realized can Harré's model be made to achieve its full potential in the second and foreign language classroom.

Mathematics

Of the curriculum areas chosen, mathematics will be seen by many to be furthest from being a 'creative art'. Philosophers since the days of Plato have debated the nature of mathematics: does mathematics imply the discovery of pre-existing absolute truths, or is it rather a creative process of human thought and invention? Despite the assumption of a Cartesian dualism, implying a disembodied rationality waiting to be 'discovered', in much of the mathematical tradition, mathematics education in the lower secondary school remains an interpersonal activity, and the development of mathematical understanding a personal process. Professional mathematicians describe their work in terms of a messy, creative, problem solving process involving false starts, dead ends and periods of frustration before arriving at the finished product: a proof of a hypothesis or a method for solving a problem. Yet Howson, in his analysis of national curricula in mathematics in fourteen countries, comments that mathematics as a cultural

---

[38] Jones, B. (1995) *Cultural Awareness*, London: CILT; Morgan, C. (1997) 'Education Through Dialogic Communication', *Fremdsprachenunterricht* 6, 422–426.

activity and component is given scant recognition in most countries.[39] School mathematics is more often perceived as requiring the memorization of facts and the reproduction of algorithms[40] and arguments continue over the extent to which school mathematics is (or should be) a different subject from that pursued at higher levels.[41] Some recent curriculum reforms, however, do identify the creative aspects of mathematics; for example, France requires mathematics to develop students' powers of analysis and deductive thought, and also to stimulate their imaginations,[42] whilst in the USA, the standards for mathematics emphasize the need for students to become confident problem solvers.[43]

This tension is apparent in the National Curriculum for England and Wales, with four of the five programmes of study emphasizing the content that pupils should know, understand and can do, whilst the other focuses on mathematical thinking processes and problem solving strategies.[44] For many people school mathematics involves pages of repetitive sums but the guidance for teachers which accompanied the National Curriculum urges that mathematics should be both a source of wonder and of delight, and that pupils should judge their work for its beauty and elegance.[45] Mathematical problems may be approached in many different ways; the solutions can be judged not just on whether they produce the right answer but also against criteria to do with generality, economy and refinement. However, such aesthetic considerations are often only implicit, at least within school mathematics.

Where mathematics is seen as requiring mainly the memorization of facts and algorithms, the emphasis is on the reproduction of someone else's knowledge rather than the creation of one's own. Learning according to this model is a passive process underpinned by notions of transmission of knowledge. The danger here is that mathematics is learned as an assortment

[39] Howson, G. (1991) *National Curricula in Mathematics*, Leicester: Mathematical Association.

[40] Schoenfeld, A.H. (1992) Learning to Think Mathematically: problem solving, metacognition and sense-making in Mathematics, in Grouws, D.A. (ed.) *Handbook of Research on Mathematics Teaching and Learning*, New York: Macmillan, 334–370.

[41] Gardiner, A. (1990) 'What Kind of Mathematics Do Our Able Students Need?' *Mathematics in School*, 19/1, 12–13; Schoenfeld, A.H. (ed.) (1994) *Mathematical Thinking and Problem Solving*, Hillsdale, NJ: Erlbaum.

[42] Howson (1991) p.16.

[43] National Council of Teachers of Mathematics (NCTM) (1989) *Curriculum and Evaluation Standards for School Mathematics*, Reston, VA: NCTM.

[44] DfE (1995) *Mathematics in the National Curriculum*, London: HMSO.

[45] Curriculum Council for Wales (1989) *Mathematics in the National Curriculum: non-statutory guidance for teachers*, Cardiff: Welsh Office, p. A1.

of unrelated facts and techniques that the learner is then unable to apply either to the solution of problems or to the construction of new knowledge.

To understand mathematics requires a series of personally significant events. A significant event occurs when the learner has an insight into the structure of the mathematics, for example, by connecting the roots of a quadratic equation with its graph, or recognising the limitations of a previously held misconception, such as that multiplication always makes things bigger. These events are personal, dependent on the peculiarities of the individual learner's concepts. If the teacher is to be able to plan for significant events that rest on individual differences, there must be a classroom culture within which the learners are actively trying to make sense of their knowledge by reflecting on previous understandings and testing out new constructs for the approval of the teacher and others. Harré's cycle would apply to such a constructivist classroom. The following section, based on the work of Howard Tanner and Sonia Jones at the University of Wales, Swansea in the early 1990s, describes a series of lessons that broadly illustrate Harré's cycle.[46]

The task set to the year 7 class (ages 11–12) was to convert fractions to decimals and to investigate which type of decimals they could make, *i.e.* which fractions convert to decimals that terminate, which to decimals that recur, which to any other type, and, most importantly, why this should happen. Students were required to plan their approach, to choose and evaluate strategies, and to communicate results. Although the task requires the practice of routine skills, it demands more than the unthinking repetition of an algorithm: the learner needs to analyse the process and to find relationships. Why do some decimals form a repeating pattern while others terminate? The emphasis is on analyzing the underlying mathematical structure rather than on just getting the right answer. Such an open investigative task requires the conventionalization of the learners into a view of mathematics as an active, creative problem-solving process with the emphasis on principled rather than merely procedural knowledge.

The appropriation stage is indicated by the extent to which students accept the problem as 'theirs'. They have to be willing to pursue the task despite setbacks and to want to make sense of their results. Although the teacher sets the initial task, emotional involvement with it leads the students to pose questions of particular interest to them.

Whilst the students were working on the task they were stopped at intervals and required to articulate their progress and their findings to the rest of the class. In order to prepare such an interim publication, the student had to identify those aspects of the work which were significant for them in

---

[46] Tanner, H.F.R. and Jones, S.A. (1995) *Better Thinking, Better Mathematics: thinking skills course to accelerate mathematical development in Years Seven and Eight*, Swansea: University of Wales Swansea.

some way. This required the students to reflect on their own findings and to contrast them with their own prior knowledge. Listening to the reports of other students and comparing these findings with the students' own led to discussion of 'surprising results', the posing of further questions, and new insights into mathematics. These processes provoke a restructuring of prior knowledge that leads to intellectual growth and promotes the student's personal development.

At the end of the task the students were required to prepare a report on their findings. This report would focus on those findings that were personally meaningful to the student. This requires crafting of the work done in the task into a form which is aesthetically satisfying to the student. It also requires self-assessment by the student, not only of the extent to which the objectives of the task have been achieved but also of the ways in which the report will meet the expectations and approval of the class and the teacher. The transformation of these events into a report is part of the student's aesthetic project.

The formal publication of the report could be via its submission to the teacher or through a presentation to the class. Both methods require the students to expose their thinking to scrutiny and possibly public censure. A classroom culture where discussion of mathematics is encouraged within a supportive atmosphere however allows students to present their findings, and to explain their methods and results to others, for constructive comments from the teacher and from other students. This provides an opportunity to contrast one's own understanding with that of others, and assists in the appropriation of what is perceived to be important in mathematics.

Thus Harré's model is of potential use in providing a framework for models of mathematics education that are more personally satisfying and productive than many currently adopted.

Teachers and curriculum planners could pay serious consideration to Rom Harré's social reality matrix, and specifically the idea of the personal identity project, for a number of reasons:

(i)   It has the potential to combine the aims of both a learner-centred and a subject-centred approach: it explains learning in terms of cultural and social assimilation both interpersonally and in relation to specific discourses;

(ii) It therefore allows for a degree of cross-disciplinary cohesion in teaching methods without reducing possibilities for specialization;

(iii) There is some evidence from the work of Malcolm Ross and his team that the approach can be successful in practice, both as a means of assessment and as a means of planning and of managing meaningful learning activity;

(iv) The approach has the potential to bring the personal excitement and
      sense of fulfilment often associated with creative arts education into a
      broader sphere: in other words, it may have the potential to increase
      students' intrinsic motivation in areas of the curriculum which are
      commonly seen as important for heavily instrumental reasons but
      which may not be seen as equally enjoyable.[47]

However, like all superficially attractive theories, successful use of the
model relies on adaptation to context. Some curriculum subjects incorporate
dynamics which render the application of the model more difficult than
others. The role of the 'other culture' in modern foreign language teaching
has been cited here as an example, and possible ways of dealing with the
difficulties have been discussed. Given all the difficulties, however, there
remain real opportunities for application of the model in schools, where it
can aid teachers in their planning, and there is a good case for empirical
testing and evaluation of such applications as have been suggested here.

However, at present, this work remains undeveloped. An early objection,
for example, might be that it remains unclear as to what constitutes desirable
identity change.

In terms of what constitutes positive self-identity, we can refer to the
work of James Marcia.[48] Building on the developmental psychology of Erik
Erikson, Marcia posits four types of 'ego-identity': Foreclosure,
characterised by a narrow conservatism and resistance to change; Identity
Diffusion, characterised by an unwillingness to commit oneself;
Moratorium, characterised by a more positive lack of commitment to a fixed
identity, in which exploration and questioning are paramount; and Identity
Achievement, in which a sense of identity has been achieved that is positive
and outgoing. Marcia notes that, in the most psychologically healthy
individuals, periods of Moratorium may alternate with periods of Identity
Achievement. While Marcia's is certainly not the last word on what
constitutes identity, his work does provide a useful and accessible
framework for the discussion of teaching strategies aimed at positive
identity development.

Marcia, like Erikson, notes the particular dynamics of the struggle for
positive identity at each stage of the lifespan, and also that the identity
statuses listed above do not become clearly evident until mid-adolescence.

---

[47] Stables, A. and Wikeley, F. (1997) 'Changes in Preference for, and Perception of
      Relative Importance of, Subjects During a Period of Educational Reform',
      Educational Studies 23/3, 393–403.
[48] Marcia, J. (1994) 'The Empirical Study of Ego Identity', in Bosma, H.,
      Graafsma, T., Grotevant, H., and de Levita, D., *Identity and Development: an
      interdisciplinary approach*, London: Sage.

Much of the teaching and learning activity that has the potential to develop positive identity status must take place earlier than this. We therefore need to look at what classroom-based educational research has had to say about identity development, even though it has generally engaged with it only implicitly.

While little previous work has addressed directly the differential roles of teaching approaches in developing student identities, some work has presupposed such a link, while other research has looked at student identities without linking them closely to pedagogic practice. In the former category can be included work such as Robert Young's on teacher-led vs. student-led classrooms;[49] in the latter, Andrew Pollard and Ann Filer's extensive studies of primary school children and their subsequent development throughout their school careers.[50] Pollard and Filer explore the development of self-identity as a learner on the basis of a series of longitudinal case studies. Pollard and Filer's four 'dimensions of strategic action' in many respects parallel Marcia's more broadly defined states of ego identity. These are:

1   Conformity (cf. Marcia's Foreclosure);
2   Re-Definition (cf. Marcia's Moratorium);
3   Non-Conformity (cf. Marcia's Identity Achievement, in that independence is marked out with confidence);
4   Anti-Conformity (cf. Marcia's Identity Diffusion, though implying a more active form of disaffection in the classroom context).

Pollard and Filer's work shows how a variety of contextual factors, within and beyond the school, impact on students' classroom identities, including relationships with teachers, but not, generally, specific teaching-and-learning events.

Young focuses on classroom discourse and takes Habermas' Ideal Speech Situation as an ideal for the classroom.[51] With respect to this, he examines teachers' interactions with their classes and draws a sharp distinction between two types of teacher-led approach, which he refers to as 'Guess-What-Teacher-Thinks' and 'What-Do-Pupils-Know?', and a more facilitating, 'Discursive' style. The implication throughout is that the Discursive empowers while the others do not. Young's model of discursive teaching bears some resemblance to Derek Edwards and Neil Mercer's earlier call for the construction of 'Common Knowledge' though Edwards and Mercer had

[49]   *Critical Theory and Classroom Talk* (Note 13).
[50]   Pollard, A. and Filer, A. (1999) *The Social World of Pupil Career*, London: Continuum.
[51]   See Habermas, J. (1984) *Theory of Communicative Action* Vol. I: Reason and the Rationalization of Society, Boston: Beacon Press.

stressed the leadership role of the teacher in encouraging 'cognitive socia-lization...through discourse'.[52] Each of these approaches is loosely grounded in Vygotskian and/or Bakhtinian assumptions about the social construction of meaning through dialogue.[53]

Andrew Pollard, in some of his earlier work, distinguished three kinds of social group among pupils, as regards their roles in the dialogue and general conduct of the classroom. While one group is 'good' in the sense of well-behaved and acquiescent, a second group is disaffected and negative. However, it is the third group, which Pollard refers to as 'Jokers', who are destined to enjoy the greatest academic success, for they are the only group actively engaged in negotiating the conduct of lessons.[54] It may well be that the positioning of students as jokers (however tiresome it may sometimes be for teachers!) is a healthy sign in terms of indicating levels of involvement that may lead to positive identity development, and this is one of several possible avenues for research to clarify the links between effective teaching and positive identity change, and to suggest improvements to the practice of teaching as a result.

However, the building of a strong body of knowledge in this area is dependent on an understanding of how learning inside classrooms relates to learning outside classrooms. Research in this area might proceed on at least two fronts.

As it is unwise to measure learning merely in terms of test results, there is a need for research to contextualize 'learning in school' within the broader context of 'learning in life'. Educational research has tended to neglect the important area of learning in the personal, civil and vocational spheres. Where work has been done in this area, such as Helen Haste's research into moral development, it has been most instructive.[55] There is considerable scope for more studies of how people of various ages identify learning within their own life-histories, for example.[56] More use might be made of autobiographical and other narrative approaches in this respect.

---

[52] Edwards and Mercer (1987) p. 155.

[53] Todorov, T. (ed.) (1984) *Mikhail Bakhtin: the dialogical principle*, Manchester: Manchester University Press. Bakhtin is known for 'dialogism' and the 'heterogeneity of voices': in other words, studies of how different strands of discourse interrupt and intermingle with each other in contexts as diverse as the novel and carnival.

[54] See also Chapter 2 (Chapter 2, Note 13 for full reference).

[55] E.g. 'Morality Across the Lifespan', in Doise, W. and Dimitriou, A. (eds) (1997) *Lifespan Developmental Psychology: European perspectives*, Chichester: Wiley, 317–350.

[56] See Stables, A. (2002) 'Diachronic and Synchronic Analysis of Education: taking account of the life-history', *Westminster Studies in Education* 25/1, 59–66.

Secondly, and self-evidently, there is a need for much more narrowly focused work at the classroom level, concentrating particularly on the differential effects of teaching approaches. Rom Harré's conception of the Identity Project can prove a useful framework for teaching across a wide range of curriculum areas. A series of inferences and implications can be drawn from this work, which might serve as questions to guide further research.

Question 1: How might identity change be measurable or observable in the classroom context?

There are a number of reasons why student behaviour should vary, and it is rarely possible to attribute any such change to a single, identifiable cause. However, there is an interest in the social-psychological literature in how individuals position themselves socially in terms of their personal development. Might it be possible, for example, to describe, more clearly than has been possible hitherto, the teaching and learning activities that encourage greater numbers of students to adopt 'Joker' roles within their classes? This might build on the large body of existing literature concerned with the development of dialogue in classrooms.

Question 2: What do we know about the responses of different identity types to the same teacher stimulus?

It seems reasonable to hypothesize that a child with a low academic self-image will feel less positive about solving a given problem than a child with a much more positive self-identity. However, research in this area is very thin. Why is that some students will find a task challenging that others will consider threatening or impossible to undertake? Ironically, we are more aware of broad national-cultural differences with respect to this than we are of differences between psychologically different individuals. In fact, there is a dearth of research generally on how students perceive individual lessons; the move towards acknowledging the student voice in educational research, as promoted by Rudduck, Pollard, and others, has tended to focus on social roles, aspirations and views of schooling generally. Although there are methodological obstacles to be overcome in researching students' views of the process of lessons, these are by no means insuperable. For example, students could be invited to respond to critical incidents recorded on videotape.

Question 3: How will different identity types respond to the same piece of teaching modelled as Identity Project?

There is much scope for case studies of teachers using the Harré-derived model in their own classrooms, on an action research basis. One of the issues that might be investigated through such praxis-based research is that of how different individuals react to examples of teaching intended to promote the Identity Project. Can such differences in response be mapped against identity types drawn from the literature, such as Marcia's? The corollary for teachers of a view of learning as identity change is that teaching might be seen as controlled identity disruption: we are all aware of the potential for teachers to exercise this power in a negative direction by, knowingly or unknowingly, branding students as failures, or even by brainwashing, but we lack both a clear conceptual framework and a strong evidence base for understanding how teachers can best stimulate positive identity development for a wide range of pupils through classroom activity, without a prior expectation of the outcomes that might arise from such activity.

At the very least, such a quest might lead to more significant experiences for students.

Chapter 10

A Pragmatic View of Learning

Drawing on arguments from previous chapters, a pragmatic, interpretive view of learning is examined in terms of its possible consequences for educational policy and for practice in teaching.

Education, like all human activities, entails a disciplined pursuit of the unattainable. There are no inalienable certainties to which education can aspire; the quality of learning lies not in the regulative ideals that inevitably give it direction, but in the quality of its processes. Anyone can aspire; it is how you go about it that matters. These processes can prove more or less useful to us practically, aesthetically, intellectually or morally.

An emphasis on process is quite in tune with a commitment to diversity, since it acknowledges that outcomes are unpredictable. We have been living in an age of standardization, however. In education, despite recent calls for decentralization by influential economic agencies,[1] the dominant drift of the twentieth century, in many countries, was towards standardization: of types of school, of curriculum, of testing, of pedagogy, of teacher education. While many of these changes were justified under banners of equality of opportunity, accountability, cost-effectiveness and evidence-based practice, a standardizing culture is always in danger of being a copy culture. We know from nature that copying is imperfect: biological vigour demands cross-fertilization, at least in the long run. Cloning, now that it has become possible, is no better than a second-best solution.

In the same spirit, education systems around the world run the danger of long-term decline through copying. Taking the example of teacher education, teachers who are trained to please only practising teachers within one school cannot be expected to develop practice that will enable the school to do better than it currently does. Schools that all teach in the same way cannot know of any other ways of teaching that might prove better; the same applies to their students.

The challenge, therefore, is to manage the change from an age of educational standardization to one of educational diversity. This requires the

---

[1] E.g. Tooley, J. (1996) *Education Without the State* and (1999) *The Global Education Industry: lessons from private education in developing countries*, both published by Institute of Economic Affairs (London).

courage to reject some ideological commitments, particularly to certain forms or understandings of equality, and to absolutist ideas about standards. However, the potential reward is that of an education system with the capacity not just to deliver, but to surprise. Enterprising, multicultural societies need such an education.

While it is beyond the scope of this book to detail policy changes, it seems appropriate to consider the move to diversity briefly under two broad headings: educational institutions, and teaching-and-learning.

Educational Institutions

A pragmatic view holds that the best educational institutions are those that are the most useful. Most useful to whom? Clearly, there are a number of stakeholders, each with their own sets of priorities. Ironically, however, educational policy has often failed to acknowledge that parents and students may also vary among themselves in their views of schools, colleges and universities. The fact that some aspirations are common does not invalidate the observation that some are not. The move towards comprehensive schools with standardized curricula, standardized tests and standardized teachers in England, for example, was never based on evidence that parents and children all wanted the same things from them. 'Comprehensive' has often been interpreted as 'same for all' rather than 'embracing difference for many'. The implication is, therefore, that the educationalists and policy-makers knew best what was good for people. Recent moves to empower parents can be seen as a step away from the long history of paternalism in educational policy, but a small one: parents are not the only consumers of educational product . As has been argued already, such paternalistic and simplistic thinking runs counter to any view of education as interpretation, or of education for diversity. It is also bound to a worldview based on the integrity of discrete nation states, and struggles to come to terms with globalization.

In effect, there may never have been much consensus about what constitutes a good education, particularly in large, relatively diverse societies. The standardizing tendency may have had more to do with trying to get value-for-money from public expenditure than with any truly educational ideal. This, ironically, has always suited those more concerned about issues of social justice in educational provision than about educational quality in terms of teaching and learning, since a 'one size fits all' approach seems, superficially, equitable.

There are, of course, very difficult tensions to try to resolve – notably between the pursuit of excellence and the necessity of mass provision. Nevertheless, it should be possible to enunciate some principles to underpin the kind of provision envisaged here:

(i) All bureaucratic control (as opposed to stakeholder influence) should be light-touch: that is to say, control of the system of provision should limit itself as far as possible to attempting to ensure availability of desired types of provision. The masters become the servants;

(ii) Provision will differ according to context. For example, issues including tradition, availability of premises, transport links and user preferences will determine issues such as whether a small town contains one or more secondary schools. Of these, 'user preferences' can be seen as an umbrella concept as well as one criterion among many.

These two criteria seem simple enough. They have rarely, if ever, however, been the *de facto* guiding principles of any major education system.

As to how such provision can, or should, be funded, there remains a further apparently irresolvable paradox: that concerning private and public/state financing. State funding implies a need to account for the use of public moneys and thus implies strong state control. Private funding is responsive to the market, but a totally market-driven system could fail to allow some students access to any decent provision. A long-running argument in the professional literature concerning education as private or public good, however, may have exacerbated rather than resolved the problem.[2] Education as interpretation is both private and public – both subjective and intersubjective – and some people value it ('it', of course, taking many forms) more than others do. Perhaps, in a system still committed to the public/private divide, private-public partnerships are the best way forward, as suggested intermittently by the Blair government in the UK. In the longer term, more fundamental reappraisal of the private-public goods issue seems inevitable, acknowledging the validity of both social democratic and neoliberal arguments about educational markets. Perhaps only when we acknowledge that opportunity involves difference (e.g. that people will never agree completely on how much of their personal or collective incomes should be spent on schooling for their children) can we move to a system that comprises a truly competitive community of educational institutions aspiring to 'best practice' rather than attempting to implement, or copy, it. An associated but controversial move may be to acknowledge the need to place opportunity, which can be experienced, above equality, which can never be measured in any humanly meaningful way.

---

2 See Chapter 2, Note 8, and Chapter 10, Note 1. The private-versus public good argument is an either-or argument. Pragmatically, surely the situation is more 'both-and'. From the individual perspective (and it is perspectives that determine educational policy), courses are studied and qualifications gained both in a spirit of serving society and of gaining, or maintaining, positional advantage within it. Indeed, positional advantage depends on a degree of social stability.

Teaching and Learning

Teaching, as has often been said, should not be thought of separately from learning. What can be said with certainty about learning from a pragmatic perspective?

We can say that as the context changes, so do the knowledge and the understanding. Whatever our children learn cannot be exactly what we know. Whatever our students learn cannot be exactly what we teach.[3]

We can say that some kinds of knowledge count for more than other kinds, and that this will always be, but there is nothing fixed about this hierarchy, or any absolute justification of it. Current funding priorities for research, for example, may favour the sciences over the humanities, but there is no guarantee that this will always be the case.

We Can Say That Knowledge Carries With it Certain Kinds of Power[4]

What do these apparent inevitabilities mean for those who are professionally engaged in educating others?

Attempts to pin down what education 'is' are bound to fail, for all the reasons given above. However, it is often possible to be reductive to the point at which there is near-universal agreement. What is the 'bottom line'? At the very least, education entails discourse in the context of asymmetrical power relations (as, of course, do many other forms of human activity). Perhaps we should say 'discourses' because meaning is relational, and we cannot attest to any meanings beyond the confines of the language games in which meanings are constituted. The educator, therefore, needs to know what is common and what is different between discourses, at a theoretical as well as a practical level, since the educator must not only engage in discourses with students, but also evaluate students' discourses with others and with various kinds of text (including, for example, their own writing). Educators also need to be able to modify their own contributions to discourse among a variety of audiences. Teacher professional discourse, therefore, involves understanding both the discourses of evaluation and

---

[3] In Wittgensteinian terms, language games change over time. However, we lack a language game for describing how or why. We can only assume that cultural change is driven by something 'real': see the references to critical realism, particularly Bhaskar, in Chapter 8.

[4] 'Power', of course, can be good, bad or value neutral; we distinguish between power as exercised over us and empowerment of others and ourselves. Much of the work of Michel Foucault was devoted to consideration of the operations of power in social and cultural life. For an overview, see Danaher, J., Schirato,T. and Webb, J. (2000) *Understanding Foucault*, London: Sage.

assessment, and, to some degree, the (language game of the) nature of dialogical activity itself, in relation to specific issues including questioning, turn-taking, the differences between speech and writing, and so on.

Pragmatic educators will accept the inevitability of power relations, but will also acknowledge their ephemerality. Students need to be able to speak and write in Standard English where appropriate (whatever that means – I refer to the National Curriculum for England and Wales[5]), but also to know about the apparently often random historical processes that led to the current valorization of the standard form over other English dialects. They need to understand that values about language are social judgments, but are none the less real for that. Linguistic judgments always are, and always were, social judgments, though the ideological rhetoric of both educational Left and Right would not have us acknowledge this, the Right traditionally wedded to notions of absolute correctness in language use, and even moral opprobrium for those who aver, and the Left convinced that schools can help bring about a better society by insisting on the equal valorization of all forms of language, by all people, in all places, and at all times, regardless of what significant others may think.

As with language, so with all aspects of the curriculum. Among any cultural group, at any time, certain subjects and concerns will be credited with more importance than others. In a society that valorizes the applied sciences above the arts, for example, students can explore why this might be so with relation to historical context. As with language, to pretend that this is not so is to fail to educate. Pragmatic education begins with acceptance rather than rejection.

Educators can also acknowledge that flexibility, openness and uncertainty are endemic to learning, and are increasingly apparent in the best learning. We can plan for the next step, but after that the consequences of our actions become so entrammeled with the consequences of other actions that the context for planning will have changed. The more rigorous education becomes, the more prescription becomes contingent. Plans to fix education, for example, in terms of public policy or pedagogical over-prescription, are always liable to contribute to killing it. The same holds true for all other forms of human endeavour; perhaps for Nature itself.

---

5   For discussion of the problem of appropriateness, see Stables, A. (1992) *An Approach to English*, Chapter 4 (pp. 71–90), London: Cassell, and (1998) 'Is it Appropriate?' *Literacy and Learning*, 2/1, 38–43. The point is that questions of appropriateness in language use are no more or less determined by social and cultural values than questions of correctness. In this sense, instructing teachers to focus on appropriateness rather than correctness is neither here nor there; it still leaves teachers with the unenviable job of transacting the social prejudices that, probably inevitably, determine judgments about language use.

However, by virtue of our inevitable roles as agents of change, all of us are effectively operating in a moral universe. A learning society, therefore, comprises citizens who are aware that their actions, practical and communicative, affect their own futures, others, the biosphere and even the space beyond. Learning, then, involves a growing sense of *how*, as well as *that*, actions have effects. A major challenge is to pursue this with rigour, yet without falling into the trap of the fallacy of single causation that often bedevils public understanding, particularly in relation to the physical, medical and biological sciences, a problem that is often exacerbated by journalists. Social scientists, including educational researchers, have often been guilty of the associated crime of taking correlations as causes, and the mass media are all too happy to collude in such fictions.

This raises at least two highly significant challenges for education as a whole:

(i)   How do we alter a consciousness that assumes that education deals with right and wrong answers, and that 'my answers are always wrong so I've given up', to one which acknowledges difficulty and openendedness as creative challenge?, and

(ii) How do we make people more aware that their own actions carry significant consequences, and by extension that there is a vast range of processes in which they can have some degree of meaningful personal involvement?

Both these questions effectively link a predisposition to learning with a certain kind of self-image, and with the development of self-identity. One of the key themes to emerge from Jean Rudduck *et al*'s study of students' views on secondary schooling is that learner self-image plays a crucial role in determining orientation to school work: by the middle years of secondary education, self-image as academic failure or success to a large extent seems to drive the whole experience of school. Chaplain (in Rudduck *et al*) shows disengaged students as scoring low on a 'self-concept as a learner scale' and goes on to summarise how their disengagement adversely colours all aspects of their school lives.[6]

Given the well established link between motivation and learning, this is hardly surprising. Ironically, however, the current interest in effective teaching and learning among educational researchers and policy makers tends to evaluate effective teaching solely in terms of measurable results and fails to find any obvious links between indicators of motivation and achievement, as was discussed in Chapters 3 and 9.

---

[6]   Rudduck *et al* (1995) *School Improvement: what can pupils tell us?* p. 101 (see also Chapter 9, Note 3).

The building of a strong body of knowledge in this area is dependent on an understanding of how learning inside classrooms relates to learning outside classrooms. If learning is not to be measured merely in terms of test results, there is a need for research to contextualize 'learning in school' within the broader context of 'learning in life'. Educational research relating to schools could pay yet more attention to the important area of learning in the personal, civil and vocational spheres than hitherto.

Looking Forwards; Looking Backwards

Just as it has been the perennial cry of the modernists in education that the postmodernists are effectively conservatives (a charge that many so-called postmodernists would refute with vigour),[7] so many may find the pragmatic view of learning espoused here unhelpful in bringing about social change. Two important points arise in relation to this.

Firstly, it is important to remind ourselves that educational practices exist for the benefit of the educated, not the educator. As interpreters, the educated will never take from their education quite what their educators expect. Social change is neither neatly predictable nor is it independent of context, nor is education its sole, or even chief, driver. Educators should remain self-critical in their furthering of their social aspirations through their social practice, lest they succeed only in repressing their students' reworkings of the material they share with them.

Secondly, as a corollary of this, education as interpretation really does look backwards, since the future is always a reworking of elements from the past. Looking backwards, far from impeding learning, is the very stuff of which learning is made. Only in the past are there records, traditions and sets of practices on which to draw. We are made human by the past. The language games whose rules we learn pre-exist us. The future is a matter of conjecture, and is always uncertain as it depends on new combinations of existing elements.

In Britain, at least, many educators over the past two decades or so have developed an almost pathological aversion to anything that could be labelled 'conservative'. Meanwhile, moneyed parents, many of them successful in business, have continued to buy into forms of schooling that are, in many ways, deeply traditional.

The message here is clear, if unfashionable. Schools can only be forward-looking in a very limited sense. They certainly should not exist simply to bring about previous generations' ambitions for them, and attempts to make

---

7   E.g. Callinicos, A. (1990) *Against Postmodernism: a marxist critique*, New York: St. Martin's Press.

them work in this way are likely to reduce their capacity for bringing about change. Speculation about futures is good educational practice, but it needs to be informed and, even then, the future cannot be pinned down. The past, by contrast, is always 'pinned down', though different readings of the past construct it in different ways. Education should – indeed, must – be backward-looking to be forward-moving. The future can only be made out of the past.

A pragmatic, interpretive, process-orientated education, then, should be both as historically aware and as open-ended as possible. The next generation must construct their own future, but can only do so in the context of their past.

Bibliography

Austin, J.L. (1965) *How To Do Things With Words*, Oxford: Oxford University Press.

Ball, S.J. (1981) *Beachside Comprehensive: a case study of secondary schooling*, Cambridge: Cambridge University Press.

Ball, S.J. (1998) 'Educational Studies, Policy Entrepreneurship and Social Theory', in Slee, R., Weiner, G. and Tomlinson, S. (eds) *School Effectiveness for Whom? Challenges to the School Effectiveness and School Improvement Movements,* London: Falmer, 70–83.

Barnes, D. and Sheeran, Y. (1991) *School Writing*, Buckingham: Open University Press.

Barthes, R. (1977) 'The Death of the Author', in *Image-Music-Text* (Trans. Heath, S.), London: Fontana, 142–148.

Bate, J. (1991) *Romantic Ecology: Wordsworth and the environmental tradition*, London: Routledge.

Beck, J. (1996) 'Nation, Curriculum and Identity in Conservative Cultural Analysis: a critical commentary', *Cambridge Journal of Education* 26/2, 171–198.

Beck, U. (1992) *Risk Society: towards a new modernity*, London: Sage.

Berger, P. and Luckmann, T. (1966) *The Social Construction of Reality: a treatise on the construction of knowledge*, New York: Doubleday.

Bernstein, B. (1975) *Class and Pedagogies: visible and invisible*, Paris: OECD.

Bhaskar, R. (1986) *Scientific Realism and Human Emancipation*, Bristol: Verso.

Bhaskar, R. and Harré, R. (1990) *Harré and his Critics*, Oxford: Blackwell.

Bishop, K., Reid, A., Stables, A., Lencastre, M., Stoer, S. and Soetaert, R. (2000) 'Developing Environmental Awareness Through Literature and Media Education: curriculum development in the context of teachers' practice', *Canadian Journal of Environmental Education* 5, 268–286.

Blanchard, K. and Johnson, S. (1996) *The One Minute Manager*, London: Harper Collins Business.

Bloom, H. (1995) *The Western Canon*, Basingstoke: Macmillan.

Bloom, H. (1998) *Shakespeare: the invention of the human*, New York: Riverhead.

Bluehdorn, I. (2000) *Post-Ecological Politics: social theory and the abdication of the ecologist paradigm*, London/New York: Routledge.

Bourdieu, P. (1997) 'Forms of Capital', in Halsey, A.H., Lauder, H., Brown, P. and Stuart Wells, A. (eds) *Education: Culture, Economy, Society,* Oxford: Oxford University Press, 46–58.

Bowers, C.A. (1974) *Cultural Literacy for Freedom: an existential perspective on teaching, curriculum and school policy*, Eugene, Oregon: Elan.

Bowers, C.A. (1995) 'Toward an Ecological Perspective', in W.Kohli (ed.) *Critical Conversations in Philosophy of Education*, New York: Routledge.

Bowers, C.A. (2001) *Education for Eco-Justice and Community*, Athens: University of Georgia Press.

Brannigan, J. (1998) *New Historicism and Cultural Materialism*, Basingstoke: Macmillan.

Braudel, F. (1981) (ed. Reynolds, S.) 'Structures of Everyday Life: the limits of the possible', Part 1 of *Civilisation and Capitalism, 15th–18th Century*, London: Collins.

Brown, P. (1987) *Schooling Ordinary Kids: inequality, unemployment and the new vocationalism*, London: Tavistock.

Bruner, J. and Haste, H. (eds) (1987) *Making Sense: the child's construction of the world*, London: Methuen.

Buell, L. (1995) *The Environmental Imagination: Thoreau, nature writing and the formation of American culture*, Cambridge, Mass.: Belknap Press of Harvard University Press.

Byram, M. and Morgan, C. (1994) *Teaching-and-Learning Language-and-Culture*, Clevedon: Multilingual Matters.

Callinicos, A. (1990) *Against Postmodernism: a marxist critique*, New York: St. Martin's Press.

Castells, M. (1996) *The Rise of the Network Society*, Oxford: Blackwell.

Castells, M. (1997) *The Power of Identity*, Oxford: Blackwell.

Castells, M. (1998) *End of Millennium*, Oxford: Blackwell.

Chomsky, N. (1965) *Aspects of the Theory of Syntax*, Cambridge, Mass.: MIT Press.

Christie, F. and Martin, J.R. (eds) (1997) *Genre and Institutions: social processes in the workplace and school*, London: Cassell.

Clune, W.H. and Witte, J.F. (1990) *Choice and Control in American Education*, New York: Falmer.

Codd, J. (1993) 'Equity and Choice: the paradox of New Zealand educational reform', *Curriculum Studies* 1/1, 75–90.

Corson, D. (1988) 'Making the Language of Education Policies More User-Friendly', *Journal of Education Policy* 3/3, 249–260.

Coupe, L. (2000) *The Green Studies Reader: from Romanticism to ecocriticism*, London: Routledge.

Culler, J. (1976) *Saussure*, London: Fontana.

Curriculum Council for Wales (CCW) (1989) *Mathematics in the National Curriculum: non-statutory guidance for teachers*, Cardiff: Welsh Office.

D'Arcy, P. (1989) *Making Sense, Shaping Meaning: writing in the context of a capacity-based approach to learning*, Portsmouth, NH: Boynton-Cook.

Danaher, J., Schirato, T. and Webb, J. (2000) *Understanding Foucault*, London: Sage.

Davis, C. (1996) *Levinas: an introduction*, Cambridge: Polity.

Deleuze, J. (1994) *Difference and Repetition*, London: Athlone.

DeMause, L.(ed.) (1976) *The History of Childhood*, London: Souvenir Press.

Department for Education (DfE) (1995) *English in the National Curriculum*, London: HMSO.

Derrida, J. (1978) *Writing and Difference*, London: Routledge and Kegan Paul.

Derrida, J. (1993) *Aporias*, Stanford,California: Stanford University Press.

DES (1989) *English for Ages 5 to 16*, London: HMSO.

DES (Department for Education and Science, UK) (1990) *Modern Foreign Languages for Ages 11 to 16*, London: HMSO.

Dewey, J. (1910) *Educational Essays*, London: Blackie.

Dewey, J. (1916) 'Vocational Aspects of Education', in *Democracy and Education*, New York: The Free Press, 306–320.

Dewey, J., (1959) 'My Pedagogic Creed', in Dworkin, M.S.(ed.) *Dewey on Education: a selection*, New York: Teachers College Press.

Dewey, J. (1966) *Democracy and Education*, New York: Free Press.

DfE (1995) *Mathematics in the National Curriculum*, London: HMSO.

DfE (1995) *Modern Foreign Languages in the National Curriculum*, London: HMSO.

DfE (Department for Education, UK) (1996) *Foreign Languages in the National Curriculum: modern*, London: HMSO.

Dickens, C. (2001) *Hard Times*, eds Kaplan, F. and Monod, S, New York: W.W. Norton.

Donaldson, M. (1978) *Children's Minds*, London: Fontana.

Drabble, M. and Stringer, J. (eds) (1987) *The Concise Oxford Companion to English Literature*, Oxford: Oxford University Press.

Dworkin, M.S. (ed.) (1959) *Dewey on Education: a selection*, New York: Teachers College Press.

Eagleton, T. (1983) *Literary Theory: an introduction*, Oxford: Blackwell.

Eatwell, R. and Wright, A. (1999) *Contemporary Political Ideologies*, London: Pinter.

Edwards, D. and Mercer, N. (1987) *Common Knowledge: the development of understanding in the classroom*, London: Routledge.

Edwards, D. and Potter, J. (1992) *Discursive Psychology*, London: Sage.

Ellis, G. and Sinclair, B. (1989) *Learning to Learn English: a course in learner training*, Cambridge: Cambridge University Press.

Elsworth, G.R., Harvey-Beavis, A., Ainley, J. and Fabris, S. (1999) 'Generic Interests and School Subject Choice', *Educational Research and Evaluation* 5/3, 290–318.

Fairclough, N. (1995) *Critical Discourse Analysis*, London: Longman.

Fielding, J. (1985) *The History of Tom Jones*, Harmondsworth: Penguin.

Fien, J. (ed.) (1993) *Environmental Education: a pathway to sustainability*, Victoria, Australia: Deakin University.

Finkielkraut, A. (2001) *In the Name of Humanity: reflections on the Twentieth Century*, London: Pimlico.

Freire, P. (1972) *Pedagogy of the Oppressed*, London: Penguin.

Fukuyama, F. (1992) *The End of History and the Last Man*, London: Hamilton.

Gadamer, H-G. (1975) *Truth and Method*, London: Sheed and Ward.

Gane, M. (1991) *Baudrillard: critical and fatal theory*, London: Routledge.

Gardiner, A. (1990) 'What Kind of Mathematics Do Our Able Students Need?', *Mathematics in School*, 19/1, 12–13.

Gare, A.E. (1994) *Postmodernism and the Environmental Crisis*, London: Routledge.

Giddens, A. (1991) *Modernity and Self-Identity: self and society in the late modern age*, Cambridge: Polity.

Giddens, A. (1999) *The Third Way: the renewal of social democracy*, Cambridge: Polity.

Giddens, A.(2000) *The Third Way and its Critics*, Cambridge: Polity.

Giroux, H.A. (1989) *Schooling for Democracy: critical pedagogy in the modern age*, London: Routledge.

Glaserfeld, E. von (1995) *Radical Constructivism: a way of knowing and learning*, London: Falmer.

Gonzalez-Gaudiano, E. (2001) 'Complexity in Environmental Education', *Educational Philosophy and Theory* 33/2, 153–166.

Goodwyn, A. and Findlay, K. (1999) 'The Cox Models Revisited: English teachers' views of their subject and the National Curriculum', *English in Education* 33/2, 19–31.

Gorard, S. and Taylor, C. (2001) *A Preliminary Consideration of the Impact of Market Forces on Educational Standards*, Cardiff: Cardiff University School of Social Sciences.

Grenfell, M. and Harris, V. (1993) 'How Do Pupils Learn?' (Part 1), *Language Learning Journal* 8, 22–25 and Part 2, *LLJ* 9, 7–11.

Griffiths, R. (1938) *Imagination and Play in Childhood*, London: University of London Institute of Education and the Home and School Council of Great Britain.

Guyer, P. (ed.) (1992) *The Cambridge Companion to Kant*, Cambridge: Cambridge University Press.

Habermas, J. (1972) *Knowledge and Human Interest*, Boston: Beacon Press.

Habermas, J. (1984) *Theory of Communicative Action* Vol.1: Reason and the Rationalization of Society, Boston: Beacon Press.

Harman, D. (2002) *In Light of Our Differences: how diversity in nature and culture makes us human*, Washington, DC: Smithsonian Institute Press.

Harré, R. (1983) *Personal Being: a theory for individual psychology*, Oxford: Blackwell.

Harré, R. (1998) *The Singular Self: an introduction to the psychology of personhood*, London: Sage.

Harré, R., Brockmeier, J. and Muhlhausler, P. (1999) *Greenspeak: a study of environmental discourse*, London: Sage.

Harré, R. and Gillett, G. (1994) *The Discursive Mind*, London: Sage.

Haste, H. (1997) 'Morality Across the Lifespan', in Doise, W. and Dimitriou, A. (eds) *Lifespan Developmental Psychology: European perspectives*, Chichester: Wiley, 317–350.

Hawkins, E. (ed.) (1988) *Intensive Language Teaching and Learning: initiatives at school level*, London: Centre for Information on Language Teaching and Research (CILT).

Hawkins, E. and Perren, G.E. (eds) (1978) *Intensive Language Teaching in Schools*, London: CILT.

Hayden, M. and Thompson, J.J. (eds) (2000) *International Schools and International Education: improving teaching, management and quality*, London: Kogan Page.

Hirsch, E.D. (1987) *Cultural Literacy: what every American needs to know*, Boston: Houghton Mifflin.

Hirst, P. (1974) *Knowledge and the Curriculum*, London: Routledge and Kegan Paul.

Hourd, M. (1949) *The Education of the Poetic Spirit*, London: Heinemann.

Howson, G. (1991) *National Curricula in Mathematics*, Leicester: Mathematical Association.

Hoyles, M. (ed.) (1979) *Changing Childhood*, London: Writers and Readers Publishing Co-operative.

Hyland, T. (1993) 'Vocational Reconstruction and Dewey's Instrumentalism', *Oxford Review of Education* 19/1, 89–100.

Isaacs, S. (1930) *Intellectual Growth in Young Children*, London: Routledge and Kegan Paul.

Isaacs, S. (1933) *Social Development in Young Children*, London: Routledge and Kegan Paul.

Jenks, C. (1996) *Childhood*, London: Routledge.

Jensen, B.B. and Schnack, K. (1997) 'The Action Competence Approach in Environmental Education', *Environmental Education Research* 3/2, 163–178.

Jickling, B. (1992) 'Why I Don't Want My Children To Be Educated For Sustainable Development', *Journal of Environmental Education* 33/4, 5–8.

Jones, B. (1995) *Cultural Awareness*, London: CILT.

Julian of Norwich (trans. Spearing, E.) (1998) *Revelations of Divine Love*, London: Penguin.

Kant, I. (trans. Meredith, J.C.) (1978) *The Critique of Judgment*, Oxford: Oxford University Press.

Kasten, E. (1998) *Bicultural Education in the North: ways of preserving and enhancing indigenous people's languages and traditional knowledge*, New York: Waxmann.

Kelly, A. (1988) 'Option Choice for Boys and Girls', *Research in Science and Technological Education* 6/1, 5–23.

Kovalik, S. and Olsen, K. (2001) *Exceeding Expectations: a user's guide to implementing brain research in the classroom*, Covington, WA: Books for Educators.

Kress, G. (1997) *Before Writing*, London: Routledge.

Kress, G. and Knapp, P. (1992) 'Genre in a Social Theory of Language', *English in Education* 26/2, 4–15.

Lacan, J. (1977) *Écrits: a selection*, New York: Norton.

Lauder, H. and Hughes, D. (1999) *Trading in Futures: why markets in education don't work*, Buckingham: Open University Press.

Lauder, H. Wikeley, F. and Jamieson, I. 'Models of Effective Schools: limits and capabilities', in Slee *et al School effectiveness for whom? Challenges to the school effectiveness and school improvement movements* (1998), 50–69.

Lave, J. and Wenger, E. (1991) *Situated Learning: legitimate peripheral participation*, Cambridge: Cambridge University Press.

Lawton, D. (1973) *Social Change, Educational Theory and Curriculum Planning*, Milton Keynes: Open University Unibooks.

Lee, L. (1962) *Cider With Rosie*, Harmondsworth: Penguin.

Lee, P.W. (1999) 'In Their Own Voices: an ethnographic study of low-achieving students within the context of school reform', *Urban Education* 34/2, 214–244.

Lévi-Strauss, C. (1962/1977) *Structural Anthropology*, Harmondsworth: Penguin.

Lewontin, R. (2000) *The Triple Helix: gene, organism and environment*, Cambridge:MA: Harvard University Press.

Lipsitt, L.P. and Reese, H.W. (1978) *Child Development*, London: Scott Foresman and Co.

Littledyke, M. (1997) 'Science Education for Environmental Awareness in a Postmodern World', *Environmental Education Research* 2/2, 197–214.

Locke, J. (1975) *Essay Concerning Human Understanding*, ed. Nidditch, P.H., Oxford: Oxford University Press.

Locke, J. (2000) *Some Thoughts Concerning Education*, ed. Yolton, J.W. Oxford: Oxford University Press.

Lyons, J. (1977) *Chomsky*, London: Fontana.

Lyotard, J.-F. (1984) *The Postmodern Condition: a report on knowledge*, Manchester: Manchester University Press.

Marcia, J. (1994) 'The Empirical Study of Ego Identity', in Bosma, H., Graafsma, T., Grotevant, H. and de Levita, D., *Identity and Development: an interdisciplinary approach*, London: Sage.

Marcinkowski, T. (1991) 'The Relationship Between Environmental Literacy and Responsible Environmental Behavior in Environmental Education', in Maldague, M. (ed.) *Methods and Techniques for Evaluating Environmental Education*, Paris: UNESCO.

Marum, E. (ed.) (1996) *Children and Books in the Modern World*, London: Falmer.

Maslow, A.H. (1968) *Towards a Psychology of Being*, New York: Litton.

Maslow, A.H. and Chiang, H-M. (1977) *The Healthy Personality*, London: D. Van Nostrand.

Mayo, P. (1999) *Gramsci, Freire and Adult Education: possibilities for transformative action*, London: Zed.

McKibben, B. (1990) *The End of Nature*, Harmondsworth: Penguin.

Mercer, N. (2000) *Words and Minds: how we use language to think together*, London: Routledge.

Milgram, N.A. and Palti, G (1993) 'Psychosocial Characteristics of Resilient Children', *Journal of Research in Personality* 27/3, 207–221.

Morgan, C. (1995) 'Cultural Awareness and the National Curriculum', *Language Learning Journal* 12, 9–12.

Morgan, C. (1996) 'Creative Writing in Foreign Language Teaching', in Thompson, L. and Millward, P. (eds) *The Teaching of Poetry: European perspectives*, London: Cassell, 44–54.

Morgan, C. (1997) Education Through Dialogic Communication, *Fremdsprachenunterricht* 6, 422–426.

National Council of Teachers of Mathematics (NCTM) (1989) *Curriculum and Evaluation Standards for School Mathematics*, Reston,VA: NCTM.

Norman, K.(ed.) (1992) *Thinking Voices: the work of the National Oracy Project*, London: Hodder and Stoughton.

Orr, D. (1992) *Ecological Literacy: education and the transition to a postmodern world*, Albany: SUNY Press.

Pappas, N. (1995) *Routledge Philosophy Guidebook to Plato and the Republic*, London: Routledge.

Phillips, R. (1998) *History Teaching, Nationhood and the State: a study in educational politics*, London: Cassell.

Plato (ed. Lee) (1987) *The Republic*, Harmondsworth: Penguin.

Pollard, A. (1985) *The Social World of the Primary School*, London: Cassell.

Pollard, A. and Filer, A. (1999) *The Social World of Pupil Career: strategic biographies through primary school*, London: Continuum.

Poster, M. (ed.) (1988) *Jean Baudrillard: selected writings*, Cambridge: Polity.

Prakash, M.S. (1995) 'Ecological Literacy for Moral Virtue: Orr on (moral) education for postmodern sustainability', *Journal of Moral Education* 24/1, 3–18.

Richardson, S. (1926) *Pamela* Vols. I, II, London: Dent.

Rorty, R. (1980) *Philosophy and the Mirror of Nature*, Princeton, N.J.: Princeton University Press.

Rorty, R. (1982) *Consequences of Pragmatism*, Brighton: Harvester.

Rorty, R. (1998) *Truth and Progress*, Cambridge: Cambridge University Press.

Ross, A. (1994) *The Chicago Gangster Theory of Life*, London: Verso.

Ross, M., Radnor, H., Mitchell, S. and Brierton, C. (1993) *Assessing Achievement in the Arts*, Buckingham: Open University Press.

Roth, C. (1992) *Environmental Literacy: its roots, evolution and direction in the 1990s*, Ohio: Ohio State University.

Rousseau, J-J., ed. Bloom, A. (1979) *Émile, or On Education*, New York: Basic.

Rudduck, J., Chaplain, R. and Wallace, G. (eds) (1996) *School Improvement: what can pupils tell us?*, London: David Fulton.

SCAA (School Curriculum and Assessment Authority [UK]) (1996) *Teaching Environmental Matters through the National Curriculum*, London: HMSO.

Schama, S. (1995) *Landscape and Memory*, New York: Random House.

Schaper, E. (1992) 'Taste, Sublimity and Genius: the aesthetics of nature and art', in Guyer, P. (ed.) *The Cambridge Companion to Kant* Cambridge: Cambridge University Press.

Schoenfeld, A.H. (1992) 'Learning to Think Mathematically: problem solving, metacognition and sense-making in Mathematics', in Grouws, D.A. (ed.) *Handbook of Research on Mathematics Teaching and Learning*, New York: Macmillan, 334–370.

Schoenfeld, A.H. (ed.) (1994) *Mathematical Thinking and Problem Solving*, Hillsdale, NJ: Erlbaum.

Scottish Office (1993) *National Strategy for Environmental Education in Scotland*, Edinburgh: HMSO.

Shulman, L. (1986) 'Those Who Understand: knowledge growth in teaching', *Educational Researcher* 15/2, 4–14.

Slee, R., Weiner, G. and Tomlinson, S. (eds.) (1998) *School Effectiveness for Whom? Challenges to the School Effectiveness and School Improvement Movements*, London: Falmer.

Solomon, Y. (1998) 'Teaching Mathematics: ritual, principle and practice', *Journal of Philosophy of Education* 32/3, 377–391.

Soper, K. (1995) *What is Nature?*, Oxford: Blackwell.

Stables, A. (1992) *An Approach to English*, London: Cassell.

Stables, A. (1996) *Subjects of Choice: the process and management of pupil and student choice*, London: Cassell.

Stables, A. (1996) 'Paradox in Compound Educational Policy Slogans: evaluating equal opportunities in subject choice', *British Journal of Educational Studies* 44/2, 159–167.

Stables, A. (1998) 'Environmental Literacy: functional, cultural, critical. The case of the SCAA guidelines', *Environmental Education Research* 4/2, 155–164.

Stables, A. (1998) 'Proximity and Distance: moral education and mass communication', *Journal of Philosophy of Education* 32/3, 399–407.

Stables, A. (1998) 'Is it Appropriate?', *Literacy and Learning* 2/1.

Stables, A. (2001) 'Who Drew the Sky: conflicting assumptions in environmental education', *Educational Philosophy and Theory* 33/2, 245–256.

Stables, A. (2002) 'Diachronic and Synchronic Analysis of Education: taking account of the life-history', *Westminster Studies in Education* 25/1, 59–66.

Stables, A. (2002) 'Environmental Education and the Arts/Science Divide: the case for a disciplined environmental literacy', in Winnett, A. (ed.) *Towards an Environmental Research Agenda*, Vol. II, Basingstoke: Palgrave.

Stables, A. and Scott, W. (1999) 'Environmental Education and the Discourses of Humanist Modernity: redefining critical environmental literacy', *Educational Philosophy and Theory* 31/2, 145–155.

Stables, A. and Scott, W. (2001) 'Disciplined Environmental Literacies', *Environmental Education* 68, 14–16.

Stables, A. and Scott, W. (2001) 'Post-Humanist Liberal Pragmatism? Environmental Education Out of Modernity', *Journal of Philosophy of Education* 35/2, 269–279.

Stables, A. and Scott, W. (2002) 'The Quest for Holism in Environmental Education', *Environmental Education Research* 8/1, 53–60.

Stables, A. and Stables, S. (1995) 'Gender Differences in Students' Approaches to A Level Subject Choices and Perceptions of A Level Subjects: a study of first-year A level students in a tertiary college', *Educational Research* 37/1, 39–51.

Stables, A. and Stables, S. (1996) 'Modern Languages at A-Level: the danger of curricular discontinuity', *Language Learning Journal* 14, 50–52.

Stables, A. and Wikeley, F. (1997) 'Changes in Preference for, and Perception of Relative Importance of, Subjects During a Period of Educational Reform', *Educational Studies* 23/3, 393–403.

Stables, A., Jones, S. and Morgan, C. (1999) 'Educating for Significant Events: the application of Harré's social reality matrix across the lower secondary school curriculum', *Journal of Curriculum Studies* 31/4, 449–461.

Stables, C.S.J. (2001) *Atypically Positive Perceptions of French at Ages 13 to 14*, MPhil thesis, Bath: University of Bath.

Stoll, L. and Fink, D. (1996) *Changing our Schools: linking school effectiveness and school improvement*, Buckingham: Open University Press.

Straughan, R. (1982) *Can We Teach Children to be Good? Basic issues in moral, personal and social education*, Milton Keynes: Open University Press.

Tanner, H.F.R. and Jones, S.A. (1995) *Better Thinking, Better Mathematics: thinking skills course to accelerate mathematical development in years seven and eight*, Swansea: University of Wales Swansea.

Todorov, T. (ed.) (1984) *Mikhail Bakhtin: the dialogical principle*, Manchester: Manchester University Press.

Tooley, J. (1996) *Education Without the State*, London: Institute of Economic Affairs.

Tooley, J. (1998) 'The Neo-Liberal Critique of State Intervention in Education: a reply to Winch', *Journal of Philosophy of Education* 32/2, 267–282.

Tooley, J. (1999) *The Global Education Industry: lessons from private education in developing countries*, London: Institute of Economic Affairs.

Vygotsky, L.S. (1978) *Mind in Society: the development of higher psychological processes*, Cambridge, Mass.: Harvard University Press.

Vygotsky, L.S. (1962) *Thought and Language*, Cambridge, Mass.:MIT Press.

Wallace, M. and Huckman, L. (1999) *Senior Management Teams in Primary Schools: the quest for synergy*, London: Routledge.

Wallace, M. and Hall, V. (1994) *Inside the SMT: Team Approaches to Secondary School Management*, London: Paul Chapman.

Walter, W. (1991) 'Defining Curriculum Policy Through Slogans', *Journal of Education Policy* 6/2, 225–238.

Wegerif, R. (1998) 'Two Images of Reason in Educational Theory', *School Field* 9, 77–105.

Wertsch, J. (1985) *Vygotsky and the Social Formation of Mind*, Cambridge, Mass.: Harvard University Press.

Whitehead, A.N., Northrop, F.S.C. and Gross, M.W. (1953) *Alfred North Whitehead: an anthology*, New York: Macmillan.

Wiener, P.P. (ed.) (1958) *Charles S. Peirce: selected writings (Values in a Universe of Chance)*, New York: Dover.

Wikeley, F. and Stables, A. (1999) 'Changes in School Students' Approaches to Subject Option Choices: a study of pupils in the West of England in 1984 and 1996', *Educational Research* 41/3, 287–299.

Williams, J.D. and Snipper, G.C. (1990) *Literacy and Bilingualism*, New York: Longman.

Willis, P.E. (1977) *Learning to Labour: how working class kids get working class jobs*, Farnborough: Saxon House.

Winch, C. (1996) *Quality and Education*, Oxford: Blackwell.

Wittgenstein, L. (1964) *Preliminary Studies for the 'Philosophical Investigations': generally known as the Blue and Brown books*, Oxford: Blackwell.

Wittgenstein, L. (1968) *Philosophical Investigations*, Oxford: Blackwell.

Wittgenstein, L. (1974) *Tractatus Logico-Philosophicus*, London: Routledge.

Woods, P. (1979) *The Divided School*, London: Routledge and Kegan Paul.

Wordsworth, W. (1973) ed. Hutchinson, T., *Wordsworth: Poetical Works*, Oxford: Oxford University Press.

Young, R. (1992) *Critical Theory and Classroom Talk*, Clevedon: Multilingual Matters.

Index